IN
THE
SHADOW
OF
THE BRIDGE

Also by Joseph Caldwell

In Such Dark Places

The Uncle from Rome

Under the Dog Star

The Deer at the River

Bread for the Baker's Child

The Pig Did It

The Pig Comes to Dinner

The Pig Goes to Hog Heavem

IN THE

SHADOW

OF

THE BRIDGE

A MEMOIR

JOSEPH CALDWELL

DELPHINIUM BOOKS

IN THE SHADOW OF THE BRIDGE

For information, address
DELPHINIUM BOOKS, INC.,
16350 Ventura Boulevard, Suite D
PO Box 803
Encino, CA 91436

Library of Congress Cataloging-in-Publication Data is
available on request.
ISBN 978-1-883285-83-8
19 20 21 22 23   LSC 10 9 8 7 6 5 4 3 2 1

First Edition

Jacket and interior design by Colin Dockrill

For

David Barbour

and

Marc Tallent

"Only in darkness is thy shadow clear."

—Hart Crane
The Bridge

THE BEGINNING

1.

This story, with a beginning, a middle, and an end, starts on the footpath of the Brooklyn Bridge at dawn, May 25, 1959. I was headed home, coming from a friend's birthday party on Willoughby Street in Brooklyn. After I came off the long ramp that led to the elevated footpath, I looked to my right, toward the Manhattan Bridge not that far to the north. There, at its Brooklyn edge, was a factory of gray bricks going black with soot that had a square clock tower. The clock read ten past five. I'd been out all night, partying. "I've got to change my life," I said to myself (not knowing it was about to change radically before I had finished crossing the bridge). The way I was living was not acceptable. It should be admitted that this was a familiar refrain.

There on the bridge I admitted to myself that "sex"

had been central to my life going back to when, in the eighth grade, after I had crossed the threshold into puberty, I fell madly in love with a fellow student I'd known since the first grade.

I couldn't keep my hands off the poor guy. So obvious did my obsession become that my eighth-grade nun, the amazing Sister Adelaide, kept me after school one day. With quiet and unaccusing confidentiality, she told me that people were beginning to talk, hinting that I might be what she called a "softie."

"Do you know what a softie is?" she asked.

"No," I lied.

"It's a boy who does impure things with other boys."

"Oh," I said.

The conversation went no further. I had been duly warned.

(For Sister Adelaide, I've used the word "amazing" and with good reason. It can't have been easy for her, a nun, to confront one of her favored pupils with such a difficult, even forbidden subject. She had made no accusation. She had wanted only to warn and protect me. Amazing indeed.)

I lived in a tenement in the shadow of the bridge in a so-called cold-water flat in which there was plenty of hot water but no central heating. My building was angled against the bridge. I could, if I were so inclined, go from my roof onto the bridge. Of course, I'd have to brave the traffic, then climb up to the raised footpath. Small wonder I did it so infrequently. But if you stood on the toilet seat and reached out the window, you could touch some of the great gray stones.

If you're an aspiring writer and you come to New York, my apartment on Hague Street was where you would want to live. Among its many recommendations was a rent of twenty-four dollars a month. Then, too, because no heat was provided, I had a Franklin stove, a cast-iron-enclosed fireplace whose doors could be left open so I could sit, transfixed, staring into the burning wood—wood I had scavenged from outside the industrial lofts that then lined Cliff Street nearby. I would gather up the discarded crates and boards as if I were foraging in a forest, take them home, bash and saw them into pieces small enough to fit into the grate in the stove.

Hague Street itself was less than a quarter of a block long—a diagonal from Pearl Street to Cliff—one car wide with sidewalks that could accommodate only one person at a time. My building shared this abbreviated block with a gutted pitch-roofed house with dormer windows that was, at the time, then doing service as a wastepaper warehouse. (It must have been a beautiful one-family home in the days of its former glory.)

My kitchen was the largest of the three "railroad" rooms. Six revelers could sit around the center-placed table. Also, there was the bathtub, lifted on four claw-footed legs so that its enameled metal covering could be used as a surface for preparing food as well as provide a drainboard space for washed dishes.

A sometime ambition never realized: with the bath-tub right there near the kitchen table, I'd considered entertaining dinner guests by having a qualified some-one take a bath during the meal, rinsing and rising at frequent intervals. It never happened. One of the more than several reasons I'd like to return to Hague Street.

An impossibility, of course. Number Eight Hague Street and the street itself no longer exist—all demol-ished and obliterated to make possible the automobile ramps connecting the bridge to the East Side Highway. The bridge, fortunately, survived, but the New York of that time is long gone. Let the twenty-four-dollar-a-month rent give an accurate measure of the change. Also, attitudes toward gays have been radically revised. Marriage equality says enough. Since this story takes place in a city so different from the one in which we live now and since it was experienced by a somewhat different person from the one I have become, allow me to set down some incidents and tell some anecdotes that, ultimately, are a necessary part of the tale I want to tell.

I decided to move to New York in the fall of 1950, after my honorable discharge from the Air Force and a few months spent at home in Milwaukee, as well as a summer in South Haven, Michigan, where I'd stage-managed a summer-stock theater company. I told my mother I was moving to New York to be in the theater, possibly writing plays. Her calm response was, "You have a right to make your own mistakes."

My older brother, Jim, objected. He was going

back into the army, having served with the OSS during World War II. He pointed out that our mother, having given birth to and reared eight children, would be left completely alone, which was true. My oldest two sisters, Mary Ellen and Rosebud, had become nuns and my brother Tom had joined the Jesuits. My sister Sally had accepted a teaching job in Michigan's Upper Peninsula and my other sisters, Helen Margaret and Franny, had married.

But I *had* to go to New York. The theater, yes, but I also needed sexual freedom, despite my successful covert activities starting in the summer between my freshman and sophomore years at Marquette High, when I'd found in a movie theater in downtown Milwaukee a ready possibility where I might offer what I had to offer. Out of the Air Force, I was now twenty-one. I had to break free. For me, it wasn't even a dilemma.

But my mother eased my way. I remember her words: "All my children have done what they wanted to do when the time came. Just because you're the last doesn't mean it should be any different." And that was that. Still, I would have gone no matter what.

(Years later, while at Yaddo, the artists' retreat in Saratoga Springs, Rosemarie Beck was also in residence. Becky, as we called her, was a painter but also an astrologist. As a project, she did each of our charts to see if there were an astrological constant among creative people.

I've forgotten most of what she said in our session together except for one encouraging discovery: "You have a ruthless streak in you.")

Two actors from South Haven, Lenny Rosenson and Loretta Leversee, and I set out for New York in Lenny's Willys, a "compact" car, made even more compact by our stacked worldly goods sharing the back seat with the one whose turn it was to be squashed in while the other two luxuriated in the front seat, their legroom intruded upon only by bags and pouches stuffed with intimate needs, like toiletries and Twinkies.

We arrived on September 12, 1950, and checked into the Arlington Hotel on West Twenty-Fifth Street, now more aptly named the Heritage Hotel. After three or four days and nights, we found an apartment at 539 West 49th Street. Furnished (sort of), its rent was eleven dollars a week, a sum divided equally among the three of us. I was in New York. No. I was home.

We did all right for ourselves. Loretta, the first to succeed, got a lead role in a Henry Aldrich TV sitcom, then two Broadway plays and several performances as understudy for Shelley Winters in the Broadway play *A Hatful of Rain*, before going to Los Angeles with her husband to start a theater of her own.

Lenny changed his name to Mark Lenard and, among other roles on stage and television, was cast as Spock's father on *Star Trek*. (In the Arlington Hotel, Lenny and I shared a room with a double bed, and in the apartment for a brief time, before the three of us split up, a pull-out couch. I take wicked pleasure in telling any Trekies I might meet that I'd slept with Spock's father.

To calm them down I would assure them that the operative word is "slept.")

Possibly the greatest gift New York has offered me is an experience I hadn't known since the disruptions of puberty, the most valued of human needs: friendship. For the first time I could forge an honest and unreserved friendship that had been impossible all those years throughout high school in Milwaukee, two years of college and the Air Force. I had friendly acquaintances and, in the Air Force, buddies. But I was forced in all of this to be withholding. Sexuality, central to one's identity, meant that the shared friendly experiences could go only so far.

Keep in mind my "secret" wasn't some near-inconsequential scandal. My secret was ugly and shameful. It was as though it disqualified me from inclusion in the human family. Believe me, please; this is not an exaggeration. We had all been condemned by no less than the inerrant word of God. (See Leviticus, Sodom and Gomorrah, and possibly Saint Paul.) We were abominations, repellent and beyond rescue. No wonder that we clung so close to each other. Who else would have us?

My secret therefore was an insurmountable barrier to the easy intimacy between "best friends." The openness, the accessibility, the emotional generosity were restricted within very specific bounds that could never be crossed—until I came to New York.

Lenny introduced me to his WWII army friends,

Roy and Marie Poole. They took me to a party where I met Don Wagner. Don Wagner took me, at another time, to a gay bar. I met Douglas Brabizon, an Englishman. I went home with him. His roommate was Basil Howes, an English actor who had come over here as understudy for a lead in a Broadway play. Basil took me to a party. I met Jimmy Throneberg. Jimmy later introduced me to my first gay couple, Roddy and Diffy. He also introduced me to the poet, Howard Moss. Howard introduced me to Van Varner and Eddy Parone. Eddy introduced me to the playwright and novelist, Jess Gregg. Starting with Jimmy, I have named those who would become my closest best friends until death us did part.

From the beginning, Roddy and Diffy (Robert Rademacher and Robert Diffenderfer) invited me to dinners that were made significant by our conversations. With them I could talk about the opera, the theater, the ballet, concerts. And sex. They defined for me the word "sophistication."

They had cocktail parties, that vanished institution (or am I just not that popular anymore?).

But these were hardly the most important elements that nourished our growing friendships. There was, of course, the secret society in which we'd all been enrolled at birth, but, looking back, I realize that it was, to our mutual good fortune, books more than anything that bound (no pun intended) us to each other—what we read, what we admired, what we discussed.

Long, long—possibly centuries before—the historic

JOSEPH CALDWELL

Supreme Court ruling of *Brown v. The Board of Education*, integrating American schools, the secret society in which I'd been enrolled as a defining component of my birthright was fully integrated. Would that the country that gave me unquestioned citizenship were equally diverse and nondiscriminatory as was—as is—the gay community.

For me, the poster boy for this claim was Jimmy Throneberg. During the time in which he was a highly active participant in the club, he had extended alliances with, in sequence, a black ballet dancer, Louis; an Asian, Susumo; and a Mexican Indian, improbably named Stephen.

My own experience of diversity is somewhat feeble if nonetheless memorable. For a brief period in the mid–nineteen fifties, I was part of a quartet loosely formed around another Jimmy, Jimmy Baldwin. (Pardon me if I can't use the more respectful "James." That wasn't the name I knew him by.)

Included in the quartet were Themistocles Hoetis, who'd already had a novel published, and Peter Panos, a Greek-American painter considered at the time to be ascendant, which, by our reckoning, we all were. Jimmy had, in addition to shorter magazine pieces, a novel published by Knopf, *Go Tell It on the Mountain*. My own inclusion was generously justified by my having won the Arts of the Theater Foundation Award for my first full-length play, *The Bridge*, about which more later.

In no way was this assemblage central to Jimmy's

life at the time. Quite possibly it was a respite from the more important intensities such as his love life and his career. It was Themistocles who introduced me to Jimmy at the San Remo—long gone—a bohemian hangout on the corner of MacDougal and Bleecker Streets in the Village (where I sometimes played word games with the lifelong lover of the poet W. H. Auden, Chester Kallman).

When I mentioned to Jimmy that I had come to New York to distance myself from family restrictions and obligations, I asked him where could he possibly go when he was already in New York. Jimmy: "I go to Paris." The other response—which should have been enraging but was said with a laugh: "When a cop tells me to move, *I move!*"

Usually the four of us would gather at Hague Street, then go to a bar on Park Row, just below Chinatown, called O'Rourke's. There were stained-glass windows. Behind the long and sparsely inhabited bar was what was reputed to be Al Smith's brown derby. Also, a large glass receptacle filled with peeled hard-boiled eggs, a concession to the law that required food to be available in all places where alcohol was being served. Especially enjoyable was a sizable school bell with a long string that the amiable woman who tended bar would pull whenever she got a tip.

Our choice of O'Rourke's was largely influenced by its low prices (a glass of beer was a dime) and its insidious and most welcome practice of—from time to time—giving us a free round, the welcome part. The insidious part was an unspoken protocol: the house never buys the last round. At least one more beer was required, with no resistance from any of us.

Against the southern wall was an upright piano known for its habitual silence. One evening, however, a woman, beautifully gowned, came in, sat down, played some Chopin, got up, and left to our perplexed applause—which went completely unacknowledged.

Somewhere along the line Jimmy gave me a copy of his play that had been informed by his evangelical childhood, *The Amen Corner*. It was thrilling and could only have been written by Jimmy—the first sign of a worthy work. A large portion of my response was envy at his ability to find the lyricism that is innate in colloquial African-American speech.

Although the play had its premiere at Howard University, in Washington, D.C., it wasn't until a decade later that it was finally given a somewhat threadbare production on Broadway, but with a stunning performance by the great African-American actress, Beah Richards, an artist who, for obvious reasons, never experienced the major career her gifts deserved.

Jimmy, during all this, was writing *Giovanni's Room*, his second novel. Just like *Go Tell It on the Mountain*, it is beautifully written, and its publication announced the arrival of an exceptional talent, even if some of the critics failed to recognize this simple truth.

In this second novel the main character is a gay

white man. Ultimately, time would prove that even with the book's gay prominence, it was the "white" presence that was more important.

Jimmy was making no secret of his determination that he not be categorized as "a Negro writer," which he considered an imposed limitation he had no intention of obliging. History, however, had other plans. And Jimmy, in the racial ferment roiling the country, fulfilled those plans with the full force of his genius, descending into the depths of our human nature and searching out all the truths that had to be applied to any understanding of the complexities—ultimately very simple—that had corrupted our country from its beginning.

But all of this was to come after our brief time together. Close to the end, rumor reached us that Judy Garland's recently released epic movie, *A Star Is Born*, was going to be cut to accommodate the attention span of straight moviegoers.

To assert our gay credentials, Jimmy and I went the next afternoon to the Paramount on Broadway before the mutilation could be inflicted. At the movie's end, I was in a state of near emotional collapse. Judy and I, after all, had been through so much together, starting with her being born in a trunk in the Princess Theater in Pocatello, Idaho, through her much impeded climb to fame, her great success, and her great love for her husband, then his death, followed by the climactic moment when, for all the world to hear, she proclaimed that immortal line, originally written by Dorothy Parker and her then husband—yes, *that* Dorothy Parker—"This is Mrs. Norman Maine." It was Jimmy to the rescue. With his right hand circling my left forearm, he guided me to Ralph's restaurant on Forty-Fifth Street—also long gone—and bought me the needed drink at the bar.

Not long after, Jimmy's other involvements began to claim more and more of his attention, including the relationship with his great and often uncooperative lover, Lucien, whom he'd met in Paris and who at varying intervals managed to accrue three wives and two children. We remaining members of the quartet, Themistocles, Peter and I, without realizing it, gradually disbanded. Without Jimmy, we had no sense of purpose. But I will always remember and cherish what Jimmy and I had achieved together: Mrs. Norman Maine, reducing me to a puddle notwithstanding, we made each other laugh. As a matter of fact, by the time Jimmy and I vacated the bar at Ralph's, Jimmy had me laughing at my somewhat excessive response to the movie.

But I was not thinking of Jimmy on May 25, 1959, as I continued the slow rise to the middle of the Brooklyn Bridge. I could see coming toward me from the bridge's Manhattan side a young man wearing chinos and a white shirt with long sleeves, and an unbuttoned collar. I kept walking toward him. He kept walking toward me. A second or two before we passed each other, he abruptly shifted his gaze in my direction, connecting with my own reflexive glance. I continued on. He continued on. After about fifteen paces, I stopped and turned around. He was standing at the footpath railing. I walked back. We greeted each other. He fit easily into the category of "acceptable."

When he spoke, there was a slight formality in his tone and the shaping of his words, almost as if he were translating from another language. He wasn't. He was shy, which meant, by my definition of shy, that he was afraid of revealing what was really on his mind.

We exchanged what are called pleasantries. His name was Gale. My name was—and is—Joe. After a few more inanities I mentioned that I lived nearby, gesturing in the direction of where the roof of my building connected with the gray stones of the bridge. This intrigued him. I invited him home. He accepted.

We walked toward the west, passed under the Manhattan-side tower, down the (then) steps. I pointed out my building as we continued the gradual descent that would lead us off the bridge.

At the end of the footpath we turned onto Frankfurt Street, just above Rose and Gold Streets. Under the overhang of the bridge, we skirted the trucks parked at the loading platforms of the warehouses built into the foundations of the bridge.

We went past Vanderwater Street, then turned left and walked under the vaulted arch where Cliff Street and Hague joined in a cul-de-sac, where a fading sign declared the presence of "Jos. Vidootsky, Herring Importers." Then a quick turn to the right where could be seen the only slanted cellar door I've ever seen in Manhattan. That was my building.

We'd been talking, of course. Fewer inanities, more specifics. He lived in Brooklyn, on Myrtle Avenue. He was a photographer. He'd just completed a project: a series of photographs of the bridge. In turn, I told him I was a playwright currently employed by the *New York Times* classical music radio station, WQXR. He was reading a biography of the American composer Charles Ives, about whom he'd developed a great enthusiasm. I told him I'd written a play that had scenes on the bridge.

In the apartment, one flight up, he took an amused interest in the Franklin stove. But we wasted no time. We undressed and got into bed. His ardor was beyond the ordinary and I responded with an involvement equal to his.

We spent the day together. During a midafternoon sexual event he told me he loved me. A simple declarative sentence that had within it the slightest hint of surprise. I pretty much assumed that this was an understandable expression of his intensity. In acknowledgment, I paused for a moment, then resumed without comment.

It became apparent during the rest of the time we spent together that day and night that his straightforward declaration had, for him, been an honest statement of fact. He became more interesting. And he was obviously very happy to be in my company, as I was to be in his. And why not?

With his show of affection and his recognition of my singular qualities—perceptions not so readily apparent to others who'd been given a no less informative opportunity to discern my superior attributes—it became apparent that I had never before made so complete a conquest. And this was not a negligible man. Tall, straight shoulders, a more than passable face that suggested an Asian intrusion into what I would later discover was his Finnish ancestry, ancestors he would claim, who were highly successful reindeer thieves. He also had a perfect nose enhanced by a fleshy fulfillment at the nostrils, and lips of already proven capabilities. I reveled in it all, accepting it as my due. I was being recognized at last for who and what I truly was.

I gave him a key to my apartment; he gave me a key to his, as well as a key to his downstairs hall. (My downstairs hall had not been deemed worthy of a lock. Remember, my rent was twenty-four dollars a month—a just and fair amount.)

On weekdays we went to our respective jobs—I to WQXR, Gale to a studio near Gramercy Park where he worked as an assistant to a Broadway set designer. I'd gotten my job at the radio station through the head of "Continuity," the designated word for the scripted commentary that was written to introduce the music. The man admired my plays that he'd read and knew of my enthusiasm about and knowledge of opera and classical music. He offered me an opportunity to work as a temp during the summer vacations of the other writers: two fledgling composers and two music majors. My work was sufficiently appreciated that I was then given a permanent job.

Evenings and weekends Gale and I were together in his or my apartment. He lived above a butcher shop, a floor-through, with the front windows facing Myrtle Avenue and the El. The El itself was exotic to say the least. Some of the cars were so ancient as to be made of wood and the windows could be opened. Also, there was a conductor to collect tickets. No less memorable, Gale would unfailingly be straddling the middle front window of his apartment waiting for me to arrive. He would also be there to see me off when I took the train either to work or to my apartment.

We went for walks. To Central Park, to Fort Greene Park, where he showed me the monument to those who, in our Revolutionary War, were imprisoned on ships in New York harbor, where the British, with their customary imperial response to discontent, left the captured soldiers to die of either starvation, sickness, or, not unlikely, suffocation.

We checked out the name on a mailbox on Cumberland Avenue—the poet, Marianne Moore, a favorite of both of us. Keep in mind that all of this was really a part of our lovemaking. We went to see Ethel Merman in *Gypsy* and came away ecstatic. We went to the City Ballet for the first performance of Balanchine's *Episodes*. In *Episode I*, a Martha Graham dancer, Paul

Taylor, danced the male lead. *Episode II* was Martha in her newly choreographed dramatization of incidents in the life of Mary, Queen of Scots. A slight note of tension: Gale responded with great enthusiasm to the Balanchine, but scorned Martha. Hers was, in fact, a decidedly inferior work, but I was a devoted acolyte and bristled, especially since I was less than enthralled with *Episode I*. (On later viewings, with Martha's contribution removed, I changed my mind. I was not at the time, however, receptive to contradiction, but I managed not to press my case.)

Gale was a well-informed advocate of contemporary music. He would play recordings, and I readily found his enthusiasm contagious. I came to appreciate the angularity, the ferocity, the revelatory sense of discovery, to say nothing of the composers' assault on those more readily accepted forms—harmony, and melody—which had been for me my earliest interests. I had for years been well primed and even eager to be receptive to all that was being offered.

At the age of four or five, I became aware that there existed a kind of music that had a different effect on me than the usual fare offered on the radio and in movie musicals. It was when I heard on the radio what the announcer called "Handel's Largo"—actually an orchestration of the aria *"Ombra mai fù"* from the composer's opera *Xerxes* (or in the Italian that had never admitted the letter x into its alphabet, *Serse*). Listening

to it, I felt what I can only describe as a sense of nobility. Yes, I felt noble. I had never felt noble before. I did
not know until that moment that I possessed the nobility that was now being revealed to me. Further, within
that nobility was—for whatever reason—a sad dignity
that deepened my response and my sense of myself. (I
felt this even years later when I discovered that this pro-
found influence in my life was occasioned by, no less, a
mezzo-soprano's or alto's apostrophe to a tree. Oh well. I,
rather than the tree, am the greater beneficiary.)

Later, when my oldest sister, Mary Ellen, demanded
quiet in the house as she went about her Saturday chores
while listening to the opera broadcast from New York,
I protested. I complained. I rebelled. The opera was all
meaningless and unending and indecipherable cater-
wauling—a word unknown to me at the time. My sister
would offer some explanation or instruction but I used
the information to repeatedly ask, "Is she dead yet?"

"No, she's not dead yet. So be quiet."

As the years went by, when the winter Saturday afternoons often cast a shadow on the high-piled, soot-
stained snow outside, I began to become more attentive. First, there was the applause, the shouting. It gave
what had preceded it a retroactive value. What could
excite an enthusiasm that bordered on pandemonium?
Then I began to hear some of the arias, explained by
Mary Ellen. Then I became aware of certain singers.
The name of Caruso—dead by then—was known to
everyone and revered. But these singers were alive and

singing. Rosa Ponselle, Lily Pons, Giovanni Martelli, Lauritz Melchior, James Melton. Then, too, I became aware—thanks to the inimitable commentator, Milton Cross—of the plots. Thwarted love, death, and anguish beyond bearing. What's not to like?

Then came the Sunday broadcast from Carnegie Hall in New York City. On Mondays, the Firestone Hour (a half hour) and the Bell Telephone Hour (the other half hour). The Longines Symphonette conducted by Mishel Piastro on Thursday. I couldn't wait. Jack Benny, the Hit Parade, Lux Radio Theater began to lose prominence.

In New York, along with some close friends I formed a cult that worshipped the great Swedish tenor, Jussi Bjoerling, to us the reigning tenor at the Met. Eventually, our most exclusive ritual was our observation of his birthday, February 2. One of us—usually Diffy or I— would cook and invite the initiated for dinner during which we would not converse but would spend the entire evening listening to his incomparable recordings. Very seldom would our vow of silence be broken.

My intimate devotion to Bjoerling found its fulfillment at his death. When I came to work on September 9, 1960, I was told he had died the night before. I was devastated. I was his most devoted champion. A memorial broadcast was scheduled for that evening. I asked the program director if I could select the arias, and write the text. So there I was in the enviable position of being allowed to pay a national tribute to the man whose art had thrilled me for all those years.

I started with *"Non piangere Lui"* from a recent-ly released recording of Puccini's *Turandot*. I included *"Che gelida manina"* from one of his signature roles, Rodolfo, in *La Bohème*. Also, *"Amor ti vieta"* from *Fedora* and a few more arias, ending with another aria from *Turandot "Nessun dorma"* ("None shall sleep").

As a concession to the tears freely flowing that morning, the continuity editor allowed me to include in my introduction a word previously forbidden because it violated the station's neutrality: "greatest." Here are the first words: "This morning on the island of Siarö, off the coast of Sweden, the greatest lyric tenor of our time, Jussi Bjoerling, died."

That evening those of us who had celebrated his birthdays listened to the program together. In silence.

In the earlier days of our relationship, Gale, too, was advancing to an even more specialized and adventur-ous appreciation of music. As I mentioned, his great enthusiasm when we met was not just for classical, but for new and contemporary work. Whatever was emerg-ing in the world of music was of immediate interest to him. He introduced me to Piston, Sessions, Stock-hausen, Carter—and his then current hero, Charles Ives. What I heard seemed, at first, to be undisciplined and arbitrary cacophony—a willful descent into chaos. The more I listened, the more I came to accept and even admire what I was hearing. Here was an emotional life that could find expression in no other way. The wilder the seeming cacophony, the greater the excitement. The boundaries seemed now to be extended considerably. The explorations, the discoveries could be endless.

Not surprisingly, I was given a particularly heavy dose of Mr. Ives. Gale, as I mentioned, was reading a recently published biography by Frances and Henry Cowell. It soon became an assignment which I eagerly accepted. And to think: Charles Ives, the composer, also headed the well-known insurance agency that had operated from an address on William Street right there in my Hague Street neighborhood.

Recordings of his work were rare. The Second and Fourth Symphonies would come several years later. (The First had been dismissed because of imposed mutilations made by his Yale mentor, Quincy Porter.) Still, Gale and I, silent, intent, would play the extant recordings of the Third Symphony, *Three Places in New England, The Unanswered Question*, and a recording of songs that included "General Booth Enters Heaven" and "Central Park in the Dark." There was also a brief but charming song with a text by the composer's wife, celebrating a neighborhood street I knew quite well. I quote the lyric in its entirety: "Ann Street/Is a very short street."

Most of the composers' names were already known to me, partly because of my job at WQXR. Now, however, I became the contemporaries' advocate—with extremely limited success.

An example: A Sunday afternoon half-hour program on WQXR was called *Music on the American Scene*. It was devoted to the work of American composers, some of them contemporary. As heaven and the program director would have it, a program featuring the music of Ives was scheduled. Again I asked if I could make the selections and write the commentary. Again the answer was "Yes." I scheduled one of the *Three Places in New England*, some of the songs, and my favorite, *The Unanswered Question*. I considered it all a most worthy accomplishment, especially since it gave me a chance to engage in a bit of propaganda central to my cause. I was able to note that Charles Ives was increasingly being recognized as a colossus among American composers.

On the following Monday morning, I was busy at my desk when Mr. Sanger, the head of the station, walked into the room. "Who did *Music on the American Scene* yesterday?" he asked. Certain that I was about to be given a well-deserved medal, I raised my hand. "I did."

Mr. Sanger: "You called Charles Ives a colossus. That's a word we reserve only for Beethoven." (He pivoted on the ball of his right foot and left the room.)

In one of our walks in my neighborhood along Pearl Street on a Saturday afternoon, as we were approaching Hanover Square, I began whistling. This was my habit. Even when conversing with a companion, unknowingly I'd begin to whistle. It was tolerated at times, disrupted at others and a minimal sense of decorum reinstated. Instead of being put off by the intrusion, Gale simply said, "That's 'Simple Gifts.'" From *Appalachian Spring*. I knew it was from Copland's *Ballet for Martha*, the score for one of her signature dances, but I didn't know it was the melody of a Shaker hymn the composer had appropriated for his own purposes.

In my thinking, that melody became forever associated with Gale. With the two of us. In later times I would summon it as I remembered our meeting on the bridge. And when I'd come to the fortissimo repeat of the central theme, I'd picture the two of us, just about to pass through the western tower, dwarfed by its massive thrust toward the sky, marking our entrance as through a lofty portal, into the strange future that awaited us both.

2.

To me, Gale was a true Brooklynite. At that time Brooklynites seemed different from those of us who lived in Manhattan. (I presume no knowledge of the Bronx and Queens. Staten Island would come later.) Brooklynites are of a different temperament— calmer, less aggressive, self-assured with no need to be snobbish (except those living in Brooklyn Heights) or condescending. This appraisal may derive from the fact that Gale at the time was the only Brooklynite I'd ever known so intimately.

And perhaps because he was a Brooklynite, Gale loved our walks throughout lower Manhattan, which was to him like another frontier. On one of these walks, he told me that he'd read my play, *The Bridge*, that he liked it and felt that I was a good writer. Not content with that, he went on to say, "But you jerk off too much." Actually, he was telling me I wasn't disciplined enough.

He was right.

Another time, we were walking past Chinatown after having gone there for dinner. We could see the Tombs, the massive prison not that far to our right, and I mentioned that I'd been there, that I'd once been arrested—and not all that long ago—sometime in late April. I explained that I'd been taken in for civil disobedience. I gave him an abbreviated version of the following:

During the previous spring, a friend of mine, Bobby Cone, a virulent anti-Catholic, who was sitting across from me at my kitchen table, eating a dinner I'd prepared, said, "If you're such a great Catholic, how come you're not joining Dorothy Day and the people from *The Catholic Worker* at the protest?" He was referring to a protest of the air-raid drill that was part of civil defense awareness of a potential nuclear attack.

I let him know I knew nothing about the protest. I did, however, know about Dorothy Day and *The Catholic Worker*—mostly from a lengthy and appealing article about her and her cause that had appeared in *The New Yorker* more than a few years before, also from having read her autobiographical book, *The Long Loneliness*. And the more than several times I had bought in Union Square for a penny her newspaper, *The Catholic Worker*, which kept me informed of her advocacy for the rights of immigrant workers exploited by the fruit and produce growers, as well as the repeated times she and her colleagues and followers walked the picket lines in support of those demanding a fair wage.

I also knew about her soup kitchen feeding the needy who, in those long-gone days, consisted mainly of Bowery derelicts.

And so I shrugged and accepted Bobby's challenge. We'd go together to the protest. It would take place in City Hall Park, just up the road, across the street from the Manhattan entrance to the Brooklyn Bridge. Bobby would come to my apartment and I'd make a hot lunch. Then we'd go up and get ourselves arrested. With Dorothy Day.

I *did* believe in her cause, her response to the idea that getting under a desk, going into a hallway, or standing in a doorway off the sidewalk would protect you from a nuclear bomb. She insisted that the only true protection from the bomb was to make sure it would never fall. And, by extension, the bomb should stop being stockpiled and, better yet, stop being made. Radical but rational.

Still, committed as I was to the purpose of the protest, would I be so eager to put myself on the line, to get myself arrested, to go to jail—and for how long—if it weren't in the company of a woman I revered? A woman who, it must be added, was famous. Was I doing this not for the cause but to insinuate myself into her company? What allowed me to continue with the plan was, first, my belief in the rightness of the protest itself. And, to completely counter my suspicion that the lure of celebrity might be operative, I told myself I would never use any of the experience for personal gain. This meant that

I'd never write about it. Did I keep my promise? The answer to that you see in front of you.

While we were eating our hot lunch of tomato soup and grilled cheese sandwiches, Bobby suggested we make a pact. If either of us changed his mind at the last minute, the other would never refer to it; much less make any accusations of cowardice. I agreed.

We went up to City Hall. I wore my good sports coat and a pair of pressed black slacks. Bobby wore a suit. I think we wore ties. In those days that was how people in general dressed for special occasions.

There was Dorothy Day, walking in a wide circle with the other protesters. She carried a hand-printed sign quoting Pope John XXIII about peace and disarmament. Unlike most celebrities, she looked just like her pictures—somewhat tall but not imposing, the gray hair with the braid circling her head, the high cheekbones, her expression both thoughtful and relaxed. Maybe "patient" is the best way to describe it.

She was wearing a loose-fitting cotton dress, the hem lower in the back than in the front. It had a pleasant, unmemorable pattern. (Upon later reflection, it occurred to me that the dress was, of course, chosen from among the castoffs given to *The Worker* for distribution to those in need, among whom she was by choice an uncomplaining recipient.)

My guess was that there were about twenty marchers. Judith Malina, the actress and founder of *The Living Theater*, was leading the others, holding a large bouquet of red roses. She had, of course, earned the right to claim a degree of distinction: she had, on another occasion, been arrested with Miss Day and had served thirty days in the Women's House of Detention (then on Sixth and Greenwich Avenues).

Bobby objected to making a spectacle of himself by walking in the circle. He'd expected to sit on a bench and, when the sirens sounded, submit to arrest. Before we could sit down, the sirens were let loose and by law everyone was required to, at the least, stand in a doorway.

A policeman with a bullhorn announced that we had five minutes to take shelter. The arrests would then be made. Bobby said, "I can't do it." We shook hands and he left the park, crossed Broadway, and headed for the entrance to the Woolworth Building. I joined the circle. Judith Malina had already left and I was told she had never intended to be arrested again after those thirty days, but had come in a show of solidarity with those of us willing now to take our turn.

Two—or was it three?—paddy wagons were already in the park. The cop calmly, perhaps a bit wearily, said, "You are under arrest. Step this way, please." He gestured toward the wagons. The women were directed toward one, the men toward another. Miss Day was made to surrender the long stick onto which she'd tacked the papal message, just to make sure she wouldn't at some later time use it as a weapon. As we climbed in, with no trace of sarcasm, we thanked the cops. We were dressed like gentlemen and we behaved like gentlemen.

It was then that I realized I'd cast myself on this particular occasion as a character somewhat distant from my own in a drama of Miss Day's devising. I would now be playing an idealistic youth dedicated to a worthy cause. I would be kind and caring, gentle in my responses to whatever might happen. My humility would show itself by my amiable good cheer and patient acceptance. I'd already begun to savor the part.

Inside the wagon, after the doors had shut us in, we chatted easily with one another, not once mentioning the circumstance into which we'd placed ourselves. We were taken to the Elizabeth Street Station, booked, and then the men were sent back into the wagons to be delivered to the Tombs. The women went to the House of Detention. As we were leaving the station, two men were filming us. Were we suspected subversives of interest to the FBI? I was impressed.

At the Tombs, while waiting to be "processed," we were served from a metal cart cold noodles and tepid cocoa. By now it was late afternoon and this would prove to be our dinner. Very much in my newly created character, I graciously thanked the men serving me and, to give my role a defining line, I made a point of asking one of the servers if he had done the cooking. I don't think he understood the question, but I complimented him just the same.

When the other men and I were herded into a capacious elevator, the cop at the controls turned, looked at how well dressed and youthful we were, and said,

"What'd they do? Raid a fraternity house?"

We were fingerprinted, then taken to an area to be processed further. From the other side of a counter, a cop told me to empty my pockets. "My coat pockets too?" I asked.

With unrestrained exasperation, he said, "You want to change the world and you don't even understand a simple sentence." With even greater emphasis: "Yes! Your coat pockets!"

For the next part of the process, we were told to strip—for what purpose I do not know, other than to make sure we each had the requisite anatomy that qualified us for residence in the men's prison. If a prize were to be given for what was on display, it would have gone to Dave from the War Resisters League.

At some point we were informed that we could send one message out. I gave them Bobby's number. They were to tell him, "The emperor has no clothes." (Sorry I couldn't come up with anything better, but there you have it. I apologize.)

We were then separated and taken to different cell blocks. Mine was a great hall with several tiers of cells rising on each side, an architectural motif soon to be replicated by the leading hack architect of the time, Philip Johnson, in his design for the State Theatre at Lincoln Center and later for the Bobst Library at New York University on Washington Square.

I had not yet been shown my assigned cell. It was that part of the evening when we inmates were let out of our confines and allowed to move around in the great space, greeting and talking to each other if we wanted. I had the sense that I was among men arrested for non-violent infractions or at least those considered not particularly dangerous. In this, as in many things set down here, I could be wrong. Still, the population seemed to be in their twenties or early thirties. I don't remember talking to anyone.

I do, however, remember a young man in his early twenties, his light brown hair longer than what was considered permissible at the time, combed straight back and drawn together at the nape in a style then designated a ducktail. He was, with effortless self-assurance, telling one of the guards that he wanted to return to his cell. The guard was not about to cooperate. My surmise was that the schedule of inmate activity was rigidly specified and requests for exception were not permitted.

My first thought was that he simply wanted to use the toilet. But I soon suspected that the petitioner's true purpose was to challenge the rules. Success would be a source of great satisfaction. The guard finally relented.

At this point my fellow inmate noticed my interest and tilted his head to the side to acknowledge the attention, then turned and went into his cell on the same level as the great hall itself. That he had detected in my behavior as something more than casual curiosity annoyed me. The part I was playing allowed for no such shenanigans. I quickly looked away.

We continued to mill around like commuters in

Grand Central Station waiting for the announcement of our destination, in this instance, lockdown for the night. Meanwhile, I noticed that one form of punishment was already in place. High, high up, were some windows that opened at a slant, the top having been pulled downward so that, looking up, there was no way any of us could see the least bit of sky.

Just before lockdown, at what I insist was an inadvertence, I glanced at the young man in his cell. I had to look *somewhere* and he was in my line of vision. I was given, in return, a knowing half smile reserved among the initiated as an acknowledgment that an offering was being signaled. I looked the other way, pretending an ignorance of the message being sent. (I don't doubt that the smile widened to a near laugh at my absurd claim of innocence.)

Before too long I was taken to my cell and given the lower bunk. No other inmate had yet been assigned to the top. It was lights-out and I lay down on the blanket. Quiet did not descend. Conversations were called back and forth with no concern for privacy—for which there seemed little need considering the innocuous nature of what was being said.

Off in the distance someone was singing in a rather fine baritone voice songs popular at the time. The singer's enunciation was perfect, as was expected in those days. Song requests would be called out, sometimes with the promise that the next morning's cornflakes would be offered in payment. I don't remember which songs were sung, with the exception of the one that was reprised more than once, "Mack the Knife."

My cellmate arrived. Much scraping of metal on metal. In character, I stood up and held out my hand. I became aware in the dim light from outside the cell that he had only a left arm. Also, when offered a brief greeting, a muttered response in Spanish to let me know he spoke no English.

The calling voices, the sung songs, became less urgent when, again, with the sound of metal on metal, the cell door opened.

"Joseph Caldwell?"

"Yes?"

"You've been bailed out."

For this, I was completely unprepared. It was an unstated agreement among those arrested with Dorothy Day that they would never post bail. Had I done so, I would have removed myself from a central tenet of Miss Day's. She would avail herself of nothing that was not also available to the poor. Upon her arrests, friends and admirers would offer to pay bail or fines. Again and again she would refuse. Our bail had been set at one thousand dollars, an appreciable sum at any time.

I realized later that the bail was punitive considering the level of our criminality. The judge and like-thinking officials did all they could to discourage opposition to the country's nuclear determination. I don't remember the name of the judge who set the bail, but I know for a certainty that he had abused the law to a far greater degree than any of us.

With no note of impatience, the cop repeated, "You've been bailed out."

Prompted by the role I was playing, I had no difficulty saying, "Can I give it to someone else?"

Less patiently: "No. You've got to get out."

I got up and asked my cellmate if there were any phone calls I could make for him. I understood him to say no.

After some procedures I've forgotten, I was sent through a downstairs door. There, waiting for me, were Bobby and another friend, Ted Thieme. Bobby, of course, had bailed me out. It was late, but the restaurants in nearby Chinatown were still open. As we walked there, as we settled in at our booth, some explanations were forthcoming. My phone message about the unclothed emperor had been revised to "The eagle has one eye." (Was my admittedly unimaginative borrowing of an all-too-easy cliché about His Imperial Majesty been considered too incendiary to be transmitted outside prison walls? I'll never know.)

Before I go any further, I must say that even though I hadn't felt the least bit of claustrophobia in the Tombs, I became euphoric to be free. Free to be with friends, free to walk the streets, free to look up at the sky, free to choose from the menu (sweet-and-sour pork). I had been given a chance to realize what it was like to be in prison, even for that brief time. The knowledge, the appreciation of freedom, continues to lurk somewhere not too deeply in my psyche, rising to the surface, un-bidden, from time to time since that clear spring night.

Bobby explained that he'd been told that I had indeed asked for bail. (Other people are framed to be put in jail. I was framed to be put out.) Bobby being Bobby, his first response was to ask if he could bail me out with his Diners Club Card. (Credit cards had not yet become standard equipage for any self-reliant citizen.) Told no, he set about raising the money, which had to be in cash. These friends, those friends, checks cashed by merchants sufficiently appreciative of Bobby's custom, cash from Ted, cash of his own.

To demonstrate the range of his efforts, he showed me a form he'd had to fill out listing the serial number of each and every bill he was submitting. It was over a page long, noting denominations large and small. Everything said by any of us during our celebratory meal was a cue for laughter. What a fine day it had proved to be.

Bobby went with me to the trial. When he asked me the name of the judge, I told him, "Judge Glowa."

His response: "*Hanging* Judge Glowa?"

The sentences were handed down in another room. We'd already pleaded guilty and were now offered a chance to make a presentencing statement. Each of us, with one exception, declined the offer. One man read a prepared speech prophesying that America would one day be shrouded in sackcloth and ashes, much to our general embarrassment. We had presented ourselves as pacific people. Calling down a wrathful curse was inconsistent with our character, especially the one I was playing.

Each of us was given ten days. Then a few names were called, mine among them. Since this was our first offense, our sentence was suspended. We were free to go; the others to be carted off—women to the Women's House of Detention (since demolished and replaced with a stunningly beautiful garden) and the men to Riker's Island, still standing (alas).

With this, it would seem that the drama was over. But I got an idea. The drama could continue, as would the performance by the character into which I'd cast myself. I would offer my services to *The Worker* for the days of my suspended sentence. How could I refuse this extended engagement?

I phoned *The Worker* and identified myself as one who had been in the protest and was now, in response to my suspended sentence, offering my services for those ten days. The offer was accepted with no indication whatsoever that anyone was as impressed by my apparent nobility as I was. Which is easily understandable. *The Worker*'s entire existence was founded and persists because of voluntary enlistments that exceed by far my paltry ten days.

My assignment was to plaster and paint the apartment in which Miss Day would live after she was out of jail. *The Worker* had recently lost its Christie Street building to make way for a new subway entrance, and it now occupied the ground floor and a few loft floors on Spring Street in Little Italy. There they would serve meals, with some spaces set aside for administrative purposes or hospitality for those in desperate need. The regular volunteers were being housed in shared apartments in the neighborhood, with Miss Day and a full-time volunteer, Judith Gregory, to occupy a first-floor apartment on the corner of Kenmare and Lafayette Streets. These were tenement apartments much in need of repair, especially Miss Day's and Judith's.

Judith and I would do the job. She was, I'd guess, in her mid-twenties. Because she wore glasses and had long, somewhat unstyled hair, she might be considered a bit plain. However, to me she was soon made highly attractive by her intelligence, her energy, and her unfailing good cheer. She wore a full skirt whose hem went farther below the knees than was usual at the time and a blouse of no particular distinction, obviously procured from among the donated clothing. I did notice, however, a seeming anomaly. Sometimes, slung from her shoulder, was what I recognized, thanks to my friend Ted Thieme, as a "coop bag," available only at the coop of his alma mater, Harvard. A few days into our association I asked Judith about it, an inquiry probably not without a hint of incredulity. If there was no shrug of Judith's shoulder, there was a shrug in her voice. "I went to Radcliffe."

We plastered—a lot. We painted the walls in the two main rooms and the bathroom and the kitchen. We painted the window and door frames. We plastered and painted the ceilings.

We talked. We amused each other. I asked about *The Worker*. She answered. I told her I was a writer, that I'd been a playwriting fellow at Yale—twice. She was not particularly impressed. She herself was, don't forget, a Radcliffe girl.

The works of *The Catholic Worker* are not done on a nine-to-five schedule. Sometimes Judith and I worked together; sometimes I'd work alone. Sometimes in the morning, other times in the afternoon or evenings. My own situation allowed for this improvisation. I was currently subsisting as first reader for my play agent, Cindy Degner. I'd read a manuscript, write a summary and a critique. For this highly skilled service I was paid five dollars a script. Some weeks I'd have four plays, sometimes two, sometimes none. But I wasn't starving. Unbelievable as it sounds, New York was then an inexpensive city. As I've mentioned, my Hague Street rent was twenty-four dollars a month. Food costs were not quite comparable, but close enough for me to survive.

One day Judith asked me if I had any other regular job. I then explained that I was able to work as a volunteer because I was *avoiding* a regular paying job. I told her that I wanted to finish a play I'd begun.

What I didn't tell Judith was that even though I was sufficiently nourished, my rent, my telephone, gas, and electric bills were rapidly accumulating. At one point I ran into the lawyer in my neighborhood who was the agent for my landlord. "Can't I have at least five dollars?" he pleaded. My own plea was for patience.

One day after Judith and I had labored together for *The Worker*, she invited me to the soup kitchen on Spring Street for lunch. It was a late serving—after the food line had come and gone. I was included now as a fellow volunteer (living in voluntary poverty?).

We had lamb stew with a thick gravy, a generosity of fresh vegetables, whole wheat bread, and cups of sassafras tea. Next to me was an elderly woman the size of a wren. She wore glasses as thick as the bottom of a Coca-Cola bottle. Her name was Deane Mowrer, and she had the sweetest, softest voice I'd ever heard. No matter the subject, she always managed to sound cheerful.

One thing I recall quite vividly. We had touched on the subject of Miss Day being in jail. With her softly smiling voice, she gave me an unexpected insight into Miss Day's several imprisonments. Was I familiar with Jesus saying that what we did for the least of our brethren, we did for Him? I did. Did I remember Jesus saying, "When I was in prison, you came and visited me?" I did. Well, when Dorothy Day would go to jail it wasn't only to give moral force to her protests, it was to search out and to find among those already locked behind prison walls the presence of her redeemer. All this made the dear good woman smile. Softly.

With these experiences, my attraction to *The Worker* intensified. It was definitely increased one afternoon when Judith and I stopped by the apartment of two men, who, like Judith, were regular volunteers. They had already completed their plastering and painting and had some leftover yellow we could use. They were readily friendly and commended me for the work Judith and I had almost finished. One of the men, early thirties probably, was, according to my response to the sight of him, highly presentable. Rather than strive for an accurate description, I might be more convincing to just say that at the sight of him an internal switch flicked on and I immediately felt an alert intensification that could be used to attract his attention.

Would that I were a "Worker," sharing an apartment, a life, with this desirable man. Of course, there was not the slightest indication whatsoever that this object of my compulsions would be in any way susceptible to my activated charms. More important, both the society and the religion in which I had been nurtured had succeeded in impressing upon me an irrefutable fact central to my identity: I was not worthy to serve in the company of these enviably dedicated people.

We finished our job, Judith and I. I was in the apartment when Miss Day arrived to see the preparations we had made for her return. Without comment she acknowledged all that had been done, probably not for a lack of gratitude but from a weariness with repeated expressions of thanks, as unending, as unrelenting as the need she had for the kindness and generosity of others to support and fulfill her mission.

I settled for the honor of walking at her side with Judith as we went from the apartment to the loft on

Spring Street. She spoke mostly to Judith and took little notice of me. It was more than enough. It was I,
not Miss Day, who should have offered thanks. She had
given me the opportunity to cast myself in this brief
drama as a character at a considerable remove from my
usual performance. I thank her now. And, always, I will
take pride in my belief that I had performed my part
most convincingly. I had almost convinced myself that
I had become the man I had so expertly played. Almost.

After I had finished recounting this story, concentrating mostly on the voluntary arrest and being put in the
Tombs, I expected to be greeted with deserved praise,
awe, and approbation. Instead, Gale said, "Purposely
getting yourself arrested? And then put in the Tombs?
Over an air-raid drill? That is the dumbest thing I've
ever heard." I decided then and there not to try to guide
him to a more preferred response. Was this the first time
that my exalted status was being called into question?
That those unassailable perfections of mine were being
subjected to reconsideration? From the beginning, all
approval, all love, all passion had been heaped upon me
as my rightful portion. Perhaps it was at this moment
I (subconsciously) became aware that the time was approaching when all the heapings might have to be earned.

Which, in hindsight, introduced the fatal element
that would lead eventually to the end of it all. I began
to court him. I made it my first purpose to please him.
This was a mistake. A courtship, I would soon learn,

was the one activity most likely to precipitate rejection. We spent fewer nights together. He would plead work—that irrefutable claim that can be very handy when needed. Now I was painting my Hague Street apartment. He helped, but disapproved of the color. "Yellow is really a shade of gray." He sometimes made it seem the new color was driving him out the door.

On one occasion we were coming back from Chinatown, late afternoon. An old mansion on Chatham Square that had done long and venerable service as a pawnbroker's imposing headquarters was being torn down. He insisted that we go inside and explore, trespassing or no trespassing. Walls were gone, floors were unreliable, stairways at a precarious tilt. But it had all once been a place of true magnificence, a home built by a highly successful businessman or fortunate heir not shy about his affluence.

Still, we knew we shouldn't be there and my unease kept growing as we went up flights of possibly unsupported stairs. He loved it. He couldn't get enough of it. The greater the danger, the more determined his trespass, the more gleeful became his insistence. And then it occurred to me: he was trying to drive me away, to make me leave, to admit failure, to prove that I was an inadequate companion. I didn't leave, even when his exultation at the ruins around us drove him to unattractive laughter. Finally, he had had enough of his adventure. We left. We'd escaped without getting caught. I had done what I could to prove myself an acceptable partner in crime.

He then pleaded work. I went home alone.

One Saturday he came over and, at some point, was washing his face at the kitchen sink. There was a mark on his neck made by either a bite or a prolonged sucking.

"What's that?"

"A mosquito bite."

Did I bang him on the head with a frying pan? No. I made no issue of it. I knew a challenge would only drive him further away. And by this time I lived in terror of a separation.

But I'm getting ahead of my story. We were, after all, easily companionable, sharing many interests, starting with the bridge where we'd met. He had his photographs. I had Hague Street. Then, too, my first full-length play identified its inspiration by being called, quite simply, *The Bridge*—with the placement of several scenes justifying my choice of title. The bridge became not only a muse but, in its own inspirational fashion, a means of extended financial support.

The play won for me the Arts of the Theater Foundation Award, granting me a monthly income of $133.33 for a year. With my twenty-four-dollar-a-month rent and my necessary habit of frugality, I was able to quit my job and live for a year struggling to write a second play.

The Bridge next got me the John Golden Fellowship in Playwriting at Yale. As if the paid tuition and monthly stipend weren't enough, the play was given a full production on the main stage, one of four presented each year. Added to all this, its favorable reception landed me a television sale of celestial proportions: a thousand dollars.

A lesson learned: for the production, each third-year set designer was required to offer a design, one of which would be chosen by me and the faculty director, Frank McMullen. We went to make our choice. Each designer made his or her presentation: a Brooklyn cabdriver's living room–dining room, and, above it, a section of the Brooklyn Bridge. Donald Oenslager, who headed the design department and was a highly successful Broadway set designer of the time, presided over the presentations.

One design in particular had a bridge that fulfilled Hart Crane's description "harp and altar." It was stunningly beautiful. At the other end of the offerings was a bridge relegated to a lowering of the grid that could be used for stage lights for other productions, backed by a transparent screen with painted, diagonal strokes suggesting "Brooklyn Bridge." Without hesitation I pointed to the harp and altar. Oenslager gave his response calmly and immediately. "*That* is the set for the play you *wish* you'd written. *This*," he said, indicating the transparency, "is for the play you actually wrote."

An informed choice had been made.

I have already mentioned Gale's proprietary claim to the bridge: his photographic series. Strange as it seems to me now, he showed me only a few of the bridge photographs. He worked with patient dedication, allowing only some few to be seen. I will not try to describe them and I would not insult them by setting down a generalized critique. Ten years later, he gave me a print on pasteboard of a rising tower angled into the shadows, the strung harp of the cables reaching down. The photograph now hangs to the left of my bed, last glimpsed at night, a first sighting of the new day.

Just past midsummer Gale began to spend more nights away. He would stay in his apartment and do his necessary work. This made all the sense in the world. Evenings were the only available time for either of us to do what we had been put on this planet to do: Gale to develop and print his photographs, I to work on the play I was writing. There was no possibility that we could work in proximity. Ours were solitary tasks that could be accomplished only by the absolute absence of any other human presence. Easily acceptable—until the absences he initiated became more frequent.

After a little more than three months of a most impressive association, the inevitable arrived. One incident gives an idea of the deterioration and the impending separation. By then it was an established custom that when we were together, it was no longer a given that we would spend the night together, a decision Gale himself would make, usually toward the end of an encounter. "You can stay over if you want to." Together we might be, but we no longer "made love." We "had sex."

The time when we had bestowed on each other a passionate fulfillment of our deepest urges had now become—on a good night—a sportive exercise that canceled rather than fulfilled those urges, not a negligible event, except that it gave an undeniable and accurate measure to what had been lost and would never return.

The affair, however, was not quite over. A Saturday night in August. The Brooklyn Bridge. Pleasant weather, the end of the star-fall season, more scientifically called a time of meteor showers, when a cosmic confluence allows Earth dwellers to see in the night sky one piece of cosmic debris, then another, then another, fall—each to its own extinction. More than once, on this same bridge, seeing the thrilling spectacle, I had sometimes wondered to myself if a moment would finally come when, on a distant planet, some sentient being would look up and, without expectation, observe a descending light that traced the final trajectory of my own planet toward its inevitable end. If any stars or meteors fell that August night, I failed to see them.

Earlier, I had phoned a few friends, offering each my company for any activity suitable for a Saturday night in New York City. No takers. Restless after a solitary meal, I had gone out onto the bridge, possibly hoping for an encounter that would distract me from my present predicament: the dissolution of my relationship with Gale. I had already determined that I could effectively cope with my disappointment. I would dismiss the entire episode as one that had come and gone, not without its rewards, and that I would now simply, as they say, move on.

Of one thing I was definitely sure: I would *not* suffer. It was forbidden that I should even indulge in regrets, much less brood over a loss or permit myself to yearn for the return of the ardent fulfillments I'd recently known. I was mature. I could accept realities, even those not of my choosing.

On that August night on the footpath of the bridge from which rose the Manhattan-side tower, I stopped to look out over the harbor, an obeisance to the view I seldom failed to offer. Maybe someone would come along and a distraction be guaranteed.

Suddenly, I terrifyingly felt warned that the spot where I was standing had been marked by some malevolent force intent upon a devastation beyond imagining.

I quickly moved away, still sheltered by the tower overhead. The warning repeated itself. My only recourse was to continue my walk across the bridge. A good brisk walk would come to my rescue. Still, the fierce warning I'd experienced had no point of reference. I had had no intimations of it as a possibility. I continued to walk. Whether I passed anyone else, I don't remember. All I knew was that I had been marked for a calamity that could strike at any moment.

Nearing midway, I ignored the familiar well-loved views: to my right, the harbor, the statue, the islands, the river, and, to my left, the inimitable skyline of the city I still loved.

The threat became unavoidable. I was about to lose my mind. At any moment I would go mad. I had an image of myself clawing my way up a wire fence, a desperate attempt at escape.

I walked back home. The world and my place in it had changed irrevocably. I undressed and got into bed. No relief seemed possible. I got dressed again and went to the Beekman Downtown Hospital emergency room a few blocks away. Only one person was there in the reception room, most likely a nurse, a man. I said all that I was capable of saying: "There's something wrong with my head." His diagnosis, without further inquiry, must have been that I was complaining of a headache. "You'll have to come back in the morning. To the clinic."

On a Sunday?—a question I was incapable of asking. I was without the means to offer a more detailed description of my ailment. By its nature, the "ailment" cautioned that involvements of any kind were dangerous, that protests or a more intensified claim of need could bring me that much closer to the imminent dissolution.

I went back home. I phoned my friend Ted, who was a longtime enthusiast of psychoanalysis, with which he himself was intimately familiar. I told him what was happening. He made no diagnosis; he offered no advice. A man of ready empathy, he simply told me to come to his place.

He lived on Seventy-Sixth Street and Riverside

Drive. To confine myself to a subway or a bus was impossible. To take a cab never occurred to me. How many miles it was from Hague Street to there I do not know. But I walked, trying to be as unaware of everything around me as possible. I do remember, however, that, as I made my way among the derelicts on the Bowery, I consciously envied them. They were free of what was happening to me. Whatever else might plague them, they had been spared this and were far more fortunate than they knew.

What I must have looked like, I have no idea—the expression on my face, my movements, the way I held my body. All I know—and remember—is that a Bowery derelict, in passing, scoffed and muttered something that I deciphered as "Nothing can be that bad." Well, yes, it can. And it was.

On Broadway, as I neared Times Square, the terror lifted. I was too exhausted to have a response beyond an acknowledgment of the fact. A few blocks further on, I had a Nedick's orange drink.

I arrived at Ted's. My impression is that we said very little. It was well past the middle of the night. In bed, next to Ted, my final words of the day were: "Gale and I aren't together anymore." Nor do I remember if we had any discussion the following morning.

Obviously I didn't hang around too long, since I walked back home. While passing through Chinatown, on Mott Street, I stopped at the Church of the Transfiguration for Sunday Mass. The word "uneasy" best describes my approach to this lifelong practice. All through my experience with Gale, I had never missed a Sunday Mass. Although my commitment to him—to say nothing of the lovemaking—presumably placed me well beyond the pale, I, with very little trouble, avoided confronting the truths of my situation. I made it all possible by pretty much ignoring it. Pertinent thoughts might have insinuated themselves into my consciousness and, perhaps, even my conscience, but I never allowed them to become an issue that required serious attention. I would, as a variant of the saying goes, "Jump off that bridge when I came to it."

I survived the Mass. I had not felt compelled to declare myself in prayer an abject penitent, nor did the mental tremors of the night before return—although they seemed to be just barely dormant, waiting to pounce again.

It was my friend Eddy Parone's birthday. When I went to the celebratory gathering, I gave him a sketchy description of the previous night's terrors, and he dismissed the incident but still gave me the name and number of his psychiatrist. "It won't happen again," he assured me. Since he was in analysis, he surely must know.

It did happen again. And I soon became aware that it could happen as it first did, unbidden, but with one slight variation. The first event came upon me without warning. Now I was constantly warned, not always alarmingly, but let's say it was a presence—like a malevolent murmuring underscoring every thought, every act. No moment was completely safe, no thought, no act immune from its infliction. But I was not completely debilitated. I could go to work and function without diminished competence. The work provided distractions. The weekends could be more problematic, but I'd already started my psychotherapy, my analysis.

The doctor's name was Robert Gould. I talked. He listened. He might comment from time to time, or ask a question, but most sessions could pass without him saying a word. That was his method and I felt no need to challenge it.

When I mentioned to my play agent that I had gone into analysis, she asked, "Does this mean you're not going to be a Catholic anymore?"

A touch of grace came upon me. I was immediately, at Cindy's words, reminded of the response James Joyce is reputed to have given to an acquaintance who, after being told by Joyce that he no longer considered himself a Catholic, had asked him, "Does that mean you'll become a Protestant?" Without hesitation, Mr. Joyce is said to have replied, "Please, I've lost my faith, not my mind." By God's good grace, I said to Cindy, "Cindy, please, I've lost my mind, not my faith."

A final scene with Gale. The Monday after the Sunday after the Saturday. Even before the Saturday attack I had resolved to end the relationship. It would be announced in no uncertain terms on the Monday get-together already planned. Without reference to the events of the weekend, I would thrust upon him that most absurd of all punishments so often resorted to by those in my position. I would, in effect, say to him, "Since you don't want me to come around anymore, I'm going to punish you by not coming around anymore!"

During the course of this last evening together, he played on the phonograph some particularly raucous twelve-tone work. And he played it at top volume. It was an assault. He knew it and I knew it. I was being tested. Again, how much would I put up with? My state was precarious to begin with, but an inborn stubbornness saw me through. I showed no particular reaction beyond a determined listening.

It was time to go. At the door, I told him I would see him no more. I offered him the keys he'd given me on the day we'd met. He accepted the keys. I asked for—and received—the key I'd given him. I went down the stairs. He closed the door.

THE MIDDLE

3.

As must be apparent from what I've written so far, I was—and am—a Catholic. It's equally apparent that I was—and am—a homosexual. As I've suggested at times, this may seem to be close to an oxymoron. So, I'll put it this way. I am close to being a congenital Catholic. It's almost encoded in my genes to the same degree and with the same imperatives as my homosexuality. I could not *not* be a Catholic any more than I could not be of Irish ancestry, or than I could not be a male of the human species. My faith has never felt dangerously challenged, even by my having been duly informed by the Roman hierarchy that I am—by choice no less—an abomination.

But please allow me to interject that this faith was informed and enforced by two "conversion" experiences. It's my contention that simply being baptized as a baby and receiving catechetical instruction is not enough to support a mature life of faith. Despite my biological claim to my persisting Catholicism, I also consider myself a convert.

My first conversion occurred when I was about fifteen. As you already know, I grew up as one of a crowd. And the crowd, as a rule, was not limited to the eight of us children and our parents. More often than not, nonpaying strays turned up at our door and years could go by before they moved on. One was a woman named Lucille—a former neighbor who, in her early thirties, married a dashing young man about a decade younger and moved with him to St. Louis—and turned up late one Sunday morning alone and cheerful. She stayed for Sunday dinner and didn't leave until more than several years later, when she'd gotten a job at the Milwaukee County Mental Hospital and had married one of the inmates.

My conversion, however, was brought about by the inclusion in our family of a pregnant woman named Rosemary whose history was somewhat obscure and from whom my parents seem to have required few or no explanations. I resented Rosemary. I was weary of the continuous chaos surrounding me, intensified by the interior chaos of my secret and roiling sexuality.

At one point, Rosemary—*pregnant* Rosemary— went off somewhere. When she returned she was no longer pregnant. If the rather radical change in her condition was ever discussed, I was not a participant.

But here was my chance to get her out of the house. Prissy prick and, in this instance, despicable hypocrite that I was, I confronted my mother.

Rosemary had obviously had an abortion. And here we were, good observant Catholics. How could we allow her to stay, considering the unforgivable sin she'd committed! That I myself had probably the previous night sought out satisfactions in some accommodating movie theater or city park was not included in the equation.

My mother's response was quiet but firm and I can quote her words without revision. "We don't know that. All we know is that she's lost her baby. And if she *did* have an abortion, doesn't that mean she needs us more than ever?"

I should have felt chastened by my mother's rebuke. I should have felt shame for my selfishness and hypocrisy. I felt none of these. I felt, with a quiet of my own, only amazement. So *this* is what our religion was all about. It was not about sin and guilt and judgment. It was about caring—a simple caring for those most in need, no matter what.

I should add, however, that this particular conversion, sincere as it was, hardly replicated what happened to Saul/Paul on the road to Damascus. Aside from an uncomplaining acceptance of Rosemary's continuing residence in our household, there was no verifiable change in the way I organized my life. I was four people, each a distinct person of my own invention, each created in response to what I wished to project in a given circumstance. I was a reasonably affable teenager at home with my family. I was a popular student at school: on the debate team, writing for the newspaper, acting in plays. I played Lucy Fairweather in an old melodrama, *The Streets of New York*. Marquette High School was an all-boys school. After the first performance, my sister Sally came up on stage and whispered confidentially, "The dress zips up the back." In a way I was, in effect, trying to seduce the entire student body, not sexually, but emotionally. "Like me. Like me. Accept me. Accept me," was my school motto and, for the most part, they did. I was even voted most popular freshman of my year, complete with a photographic spread in the school paper, *The Flambeau*.

At work, as a soda jerk in Walgreen's Drug Store on Third Street and Wisconsin Avenue—the Times Square of Milwaukee—I was something of a showoff, too proud to be less than the best at my job. I was, by common consent, the fastest soda jerk in town.

Then there was my sex life. Looking back, I'm rather pleased with myself that I could so adroitly juggle these several manipulations and mysteries without collision or collapse. And I have to wonder now if it was contributory to my becoming a writer of fiction and a playwright, an apprenticeship I am not inclined to disown.

Which, if any, of the four persons was the real me? Each expressed a particular need, so maybe I was an amalgam of all four. But I must add that the secret sexual activist was the most honest, the least manipulative—qualities that I hope inform what I'm writing now.

As for that first conversion, it has continued a lurking, sometimes more apparent presence that would eventually reinforce the second. The second occurred when I was living in what has since been reconfigured into a sanitized and gentrified "East Village," then known less pretentiously as the Lower East Side. I was in a fifth-floor walk-up overlooking Tompkins Square. The skyline of lower Manhattan was a stunning view with glorious sunsets. The apartment itself went the length of the building, front to back, large enough to include a dining room with a nonworking fireplace.

Enviable as the view may have been, the apartment, being on the top floor, with the fire escape outside my bathroom window, was the prime candidate for anyone coming down from the roof wishing to acquire a television, a radio, a typewriter, and other marketable artifacts. An accordion metal gate was installed on the bathroom fire-escape window. After it became apparent that access was also available from the ledge of the library building next door, that window, too, was given a gate. Next, the two kitchen windows. Security was breached, however, by simply breaking through my wooden hallway door. An iron plate was bolted in place and a rod-enforced lock was installed. You get the picture.

At that time, the neighborhood was, to say the least, interesting. Previously a Ukrainian and Polish enclave, these initial refugees were made exiles once again in flight from the despotism of drugs and the invading hippies intent on a freedom only anarchy can provide. And yet, it was very definitely a neighborhood. Its citizenry was not limited to those mentioned above. The parish church of St. Brigid was on Avenue B, on the east side of the square. Its young priests, Matt and Dermot, had learned Spanish to reach out as effectively as possible to the Hispanic families moving into the territory. (I noticed that when they preached in Spanish, they gestured much more generously than when they preached in English.) They also tried to bring together the artists, writers, dancers, and booksellers attracted to the undeniable vitality of the area, to say nothing of the day laborers who, with their families, formed the hard core of any neighborhood.

It wasn't easy for Matt. It wasn't easy for Dermot. Poverty, crime, rivalries, and exploitative real estate gougers were prevailing influences. And I watched as these two young priests struggled tenaciously and creatively to bring us all together.

That was my second conversion. The true mission of Christianity to which I had subscribed was to an inclusive community, a community irrevocably established by the birth, death, resurrection, and ascension of Jesus. Christianity's purpose was neither the exercise of power nor the imposition of dogmas. Its striving was not for conformity enforced from above, but for its opposite—a unity from within, inspired ideally by love. If that couldn't be fully achieved, then at least by a determined caring. Nothing less. We are each other's divinely appointed protector—and whatever harm we do to each other, it is a harm perpetrated by a God-appointed guardian—oneself.

These are the truths that, along with a sacramental life, sustain my faith.

This does not mean that I don't have moments of serious doubt, which is hardly a unique experience for any person of persisting faith. Do I really believe that the consecrated bread (actually at its beginning it was rather like present-day matzoh, unleavened bread made necessary for the Passover meal before a quick getaway from Egypt) and the consecrated wine are truly the actual body and blood of Jesus Himself, and not a symbolic memorial? Well, yes.

Rather than go on and on ticking off one bizarre belief after another, let me just say this: one of the more important ingredients of faith is humility—a humility that doesn't require that everything be fully known or explained completely, making no allowance for mystery. As far as I'm concerned, the purpose of reality is to show the way to mystery, which is the ultimate reality.

One more quick challenge to one's faith: the efficacy of prayer. It's my considered contention that not one of us who has ever prayed has not been troubled at times by an inescapable thought: "Is anyone really listening?"

This leads me to some thoughts as regards my religion and my homosexuality.

Whenever I'm asked about my sexuality, I say, "I am, by God's good grace, as gay as a goose." Glib, I know, but true. I have come to see my homosexuality as a form of grace. Because of my outcast state I was forced to think for myself. The rules that guide heterosexuals were not applicable to me. For starters, the old saying "Save it for the girl you'll marry" had no meaning. There would be no circumstance in which I could fulfill my sexuality within a shared love. I was, in effect, given to understand that only a celibate life was acceptable. In other words, I was informed that I must take a perpetual vow of chastity—a sacrificial life to which I knew only too well I had *not* been called. My conscience therefore had to be shaped independent of hierarchical instruction and dogmatic guidance. This was liberating, but it was liberation that was also alienating.

In New York, cardinal after cardinal after cardinal was in highly vocal opposition to any laws that would prohibit discrimination against homosexuals. Without this law-given protection we could be fired from our jobs, evicted from our apartments. Ultimately, we were to be hounded off the edge of the earth for the simple reason that God, in his inscrutable wisdom, had included homosexuality within the human nature he had allowed to evolve into his own image.

My response to the cardinals proved to be quite

simple: I knew I was not expelled from the community, that I could continue in good conscience to fully participate in the sacramental life that lies at the heart of the Church.

At one time, until proscribed and forced to disperse by the then cardinal, there was a faith group of homosexual Catholics called Dignity. I never joined. With all due respect to them, I refused to separate myself. I was a member of the full and indivisible community expressed by my membership in St. Brigid's and, later, the parish of St. Joseph in Greenwich Village. And I would in no circumstance remove myself. Unfortunately, a similar insistence did not inform His Eminence's ruthlessness. According to him, homosexuals by their nature had no place in *his* Church. His indeed! The Church is Christ's Church and its unity is indissoluble. Whether that community will ever be *fulfilled* is another matter.

I would later articulate my insistent stand in the following terms: surely the Almighty has a sufficient fund of grace to sustain my faith even against the repeated onslaughts of a cardinal archbishop.

Sometimes I have wondered if the greatest satanic success since the eating of the Edenic apple was the conversion of the Roman Emperor Constantine to Christianity. This, in turn, led one of his successors, Theodosius, to proclaim Christianity the religion of the Empire. As a power of the state, the shifts and changes began. Power wants nothing so much as perpetuation and increase. The Bishop of Rome, the Pope, and his hierarchy had considered themselves before as "the servants of the servants of God"—those servants of God being, of course, the community. All too soon the servants became the masters. The Community of Love became an Institution of Laws, the Church's mission no longer the fulfillment of the divinely established Community, but obedience to a hierarchically imposed conformity.

Vatican II, convened in Saint Peter's Basilica by Pope John XXIII in October 1962 and closing in December 1965, did what it could to effect something of a return. But the attempt was largely nullified by Pope Paul VI's encyclical, *Humanae Vitae*, issued in July 1968, in which he unilaterally, like the absolute monarch that the Council had tried to reform, decreed that contraception was still not to be permitted, overruling his own committee that had overwhelmingly agreed that it should be allowed.

In his near-hagiographic biography of John Paul II, *His Holiness*, Carl Bernstein notes that it was Karol Wojtyla, then the Cardinal Archbishop of Krakow, who warned Paul VI that if he were to contradict previous popes on this subject, it would diminish the authority of the Papacy. So much for being a servant.

Full disclosure: The great hero of my life is Angelo Giuseppe Roncalli, Pope John XXIII (1958–1963), the man who, when the Chief Rabbi of Jerusalem came at his invitation to Rome, walked out on to the tarmac at the airport. He opened his wide arms, and in the most personal way possible proclaimed in Hebrew a central Christian truth that nullifies for all time to come any presumed justification for Christian anti-Semitism, "*I am your brother Joseph.*"

With the elevation of Francis to the Chair of Peter, there has been a change of tone and attitude that is most welcome. Particularly welcome is his reaffirmation of the pronouncement of Vatican II that defines the Church as the People of God—the Community, as well as his reminder (from Vatican II) concerning the primacy of individual conscience. Then, too, there is his call for an apology from the Church for its treatment of women and gays.

As for women, any hope for a much-needed reform—starting with the ordination of women priests—has already been declared futile. Pope Francis has publicly subscribed to the ruling of Pope John Paul II: since only men were apostles, only men can be priests. For me, this reasoning is a failed attempt to avoid the truth lurking behind John Paul's and Francis's decision that women are second- or third-class citizens and must deal with it as best they can, preferably, as the popes would have it, without complaint.

My disagreement is apparent. To make my case, a true story: When I was at the American Academy in Rome (how I got there comes later), one of my colleagues, an architect, designed as a project a church and, for help with the iconography, enlisted a priest attached to the Vatican. To thank him, he invited him and a younger priest to dinner in the apartment where he and his wife and children were staying. As one of the few Catholic Fellows at the Academy, I, too, was invited. A most enjoyable evening.

After dinner, we settled down in the living room to continue. This was in 1980, and the priest asked me what I thought of the (then) new pope, John Paul II, whose pontificate began in 1978 and ended in 2005, I more or less shrugged and said, "*Mezza-mezza*" (so-so). This surprised him. Why the half measure of approval? I pulled out of thin air the first thought that came into my mind. Another shrug, then I said, "The ordination of women. The Holy Spirit calls whom the Holy Spirit wills to call—a man or a woman. You may not tell God what God may and may not do. And if you persist, it's a grave matter, and gravely will he [Pope John Paul II] answer for it."

At this, the younger priest stood up and said, "Well, time to go."

"No," I pleaded. "I just got started."

By this time both priests were on their feet. Good-byes were said and they left. After they were gone, my host explained to me that the older priest who had helped him had been an Episcopalian priest who had come over to Rome because of his Church's ordination of women. I congratulated myself. The man was obviously in need of my instruction.

For gays, it has proved to be another matter indeed.

I was as much astounded as I was moved by the report of the Chilean victim of sexual abuse, Juan Carlos Cruz, who met privately with Pope Francis at the Vatican. According to him, it was through his tears that he told Francis that he had always persevered in his Catholic faith even though the hierarchy had claimed he could not be a Catholic because he led a life of perversion. More specifically, he had been informed beyond contradiction by catechetical instruction that he was "intrinsically disordered and contrary to the natural law." (Sounds familiar.)

In response to the man's distress, Francis said, "You have to be happy [happy?!!!] with who you are. God made you this way and loves you this way, and the Pope loves you this way."

For those few moments, the Church had become again its early self, an inclusive community of love and caring. Whether the moment expands to revised teachings remains to be seen. Formidable forces are arrayed against both Francis and Juan Carlos Cruz—those who would prefer dictated conformity and are opposed to those who continue the struggle to fulfill an inspired community. On yet one more level, we live in interesting times.

With Pope Francis in mind, I'd like to bring up his eloquent if futile attempt to convert the Congress of the United States to simple human decency. One of his pleas was for an end to capital punishment, a subject to which I've given considerable thought. Those lawgivers so adamantly in favor of it cry out for justice. I respect that, and, in response offer the following:

We know there is no justice on earth. I won't even mention our so-called criminal justice system. That's too obvious. But some of us are born to unearned privilege, while others are born weighted down by undeserved burdens that will never be lifted. Some are more intelligent, more attractive, more temperamentally suited for success. And so it goes.

There is no justice in heaven. In heaven there is only mercy. Everyone there has been admitted because of God's redemptive love that finds its highest expression in His mercy.

Only hell is just. In hell, everyone is given exactly what he or she deserves. (See Dante.) Only there is justice readily enforced. It's my suggestion, therefore, that those same lawgivers (and those who implemented those laws) so insistent in their demand for justice repair at the earliest opportunity to the one and only place where it is readily available: hell. I am sure they will be *warmly* received.

As part of this examination of my religion and my homosexuality, let me note the following: it has been a long-held belief of mine that a good argument is a form of intimacy. How ironic in a way that my passionate opposition to my Church's hierarchy has bound me with hoops of steel to the Church that has tried with equal passion to get rid of me.

An incident: At the MacDowell Colony in New

Hampshire, where I was, at the time, working on my first novel, *In Such Dark Places*, a fellow-writer, Norma Rosen, confronted me when she saw me heading out to Sunday Mass in Peterborough. "How can you be a Catholic?" she asked. "How can you still be a Catholic?"

"Norma," I answered, "if I weren't, I'd miss the tension."

4.

There were brief episodes during this middle period when Gale and I saw each other. Shortly after the first New Year since our farewells, he stopped by, unannounced, at Hague Street. Our talk was inconsequential catch-up conversation. I'd finished my play and it was with my agent. He was considering a series of photographs that would capture the vitality of Myrtle Avenue. There may already have been rumors that the dilapidated El was marked for demise—just as New York's Third Avenue El disappeared during my two years at Yale.

It was expected that Myrtle Avenue would be transformed. Why it needed transformation could best be explained by the real estate speculators ready to pounce at any moment. Myrtle Avenue at that time seemed a thriving, bustling, diverse community. It was a self-sufficient village. That this was made possible by low rents, both residential and commercial, was hardly a secret. Does that hint at the reasoning behind the piously proposed "transformation"? No comment.

Anyway, there was Gale, back at Hague Street— and he did stay the night. If he had come to confirm that our separation was not to his liking, no real evidence presented itself. He was, at best, a perfunctory guest and I sensed that the least effective stimulant that I could offer would be pleas for his immediate return. The next morning, at parting, he spoke of a possible repeat engagement. I was to call him later. I called him. We'd get together another time. Yeah.

Once I ran into him on a misty night on the Brooklyn Heights Promenade, where offerings of availability were made with little pretense of being there for the view. It was a brief encounter. I mentioned that I was seeing a psychiatrist. He said he'd been considering asking me home, but this had changed his mind. He walked away. I mentioned the Promenade meeting to Dr. Gould. I speculated that the mention of psychiatric treatment inspired, in Gale, a fear that I might have a fit on the floor. Uncharacteristically, the doctor rewarded my alliteration with a quick guffaw. Where *that* came from, I'll never know.

By the time or, actually, immediately after my final leave-taking with its key exchange, it became only too apparent that what had long been operative during the time of diminishing affection was now undeniable. I was desperate.

I felt I'd been expelled from the Garden without ever being aware that I'd bitten into the offered apple. Of course, I had not only taken a luscious bite, I'd chewed and swallowed a sizable chunk. If my Edenic ancestors had partaken of the forbidden fruit, convinced that it qualified them to be like God, worshipped and adored, I was no less guilty of highest pride than they had been. How readily had I subscribed to the notion that I was worthy of abject adulation, that I was perfection itself and was finally being recognized as the superior being I'd often suspected myself to be. With Gale, the long-awaited votary had finally appeared. I had come to the deserved and destined apotheosis and had only to accept and revel in it.

That the tasted apple might inflict an incurable malady, that the incessant longing I was experiencing would never be appeased, came slowly and inexorably as something of a surprise. This reversal seemed to contradict nature itself. How could I be revealed as an obvious marvel and then informed that a terrible mistake had been made? And not only must I now survive the expulsion but be forced to remember my former estate and, worst of all, yearn with an exile's yearning for a return that would never be allowed.

5.

Dr. Gould's office was on Gramercy Park in a building of medieval pretensions, typified by the two more-than-life-size statues in knightly armor that guarded the entryway. Our sessions took place in the unimpressive living room of an apartment on the first floor, to the right after I had come into the building. Near windows that looked out onto the park, he sat in one chair, facing me, and I, in another across the room, facing him. The chairs were comfortable but designed more for support than for relaxation.

Dr. Gould, I would say, was in his late thirties, slender, not muscular. His hair was medium brown, close to a crewcut. His features were well defined and seemed to feel no need to be imposing. His was a reasonably good-looking face, his expressions professionally noncommittal, his demeanor attentive without seeming intensely engaged.

I remember mostly short-sleeved shirts, slacks, brown sandals and tan socks—this latter easily remembered since I spent a considerable amount of time staring at them while struggling to get out what I was trying to uncover. During moments of uncertain articulation, I would stare at a tree across the street. Not infrequently, I looked directly at my analyst—for the simple reason that he was the person I was talking to, and he was right there across from me.

At our first session I told him of the breakup with Gale, of the episode on the bridge where I had realized that my mind was being threatened, and of my continuing fear that the assault might be repeated. I remember no questions that he may have asked. He required that I do the talking—and very rarely would he either question or comment. At the start I decided: I would never lie to him. This was prompted not by a preference for the truth and nothing but the truth, but for two reasons: What was the point of therapy if I was going to lie my way out of difficult admissions or untenable discoveries? A more active motive: I believed (accurately or not) that he would know when I was lying and, like all liars, I didn't want to be caught in the act.

Strangely enough, the episode on the bridge, the terror that had forced me to seek the help I was supposedly there to receive, was not to be allotted the pride of place during our early sessions. Gale, homosexuality, desperation, loss, and my feelings and understandings regarding them were obviously more important. (It is a measure of my inability to understand myself that I would realize much later that my separation from Gale in no way caused the assault. But the good doctor required me for the most part to set the agenda and also the course we would travel together.)

Early on I told Dr. Gould about my stint with *The Catholic Worker*, and he asked me why I felt so drawn to Miss Day and the organization. I told him it possibly had to do with having been poor for a time during childhood. I explained how, one day on my way to school (I was a fifth grader at the time), I said to myself with quiet surprise, "I'm hungry." I don't remember what I'd been given for lunch, but it hadn't been enough. Also, I couldn't remember the last time I'd had any fresh fruit. It was borne home to me at that moment that we, my family and I, were poor, which, at an earlier time, was a designation reserved for others, a class that existed at a safe remove even when they lived in close proximity—like the Millers down the block or fellow students at school whose families were on "relief"—an inadequate sustenance that humiliated as much as it helped.

My family was made poor not by the debilitating Depression but by a bureaucratic fiat that decreed my father's retirement from his job at the Post Office at the age of sixty-five. For many employees this would be a well-earned reward for years of faithful service. For many, but not for my father. He had been the youngest of nine children and, in the memory implanted during my early years, had been, as the youngest, the designated caregiver and possibly the main support for his aging parents. (His father lived to ninety-two.) My father was able to marry for the first and only time at the age of forty-four, which in itself, for a first-generation American of Irish descent, was not all that unusual. What created a category distinctive to himself was his unimpeded procreation of eight children within the next eleven years. Which means that at age sixty-five he still had a young family to feed, clothe, shelter, and educate—all with a pension: one half of his previous salary. We were provided with enough, if not to live on, to make us ineligible for any public assistance.

A further difficulty contributed to our predicament. My father, humiliated by his failure to adequately provide for his family, became a drunk for almost two years. My tattered clothes, shoes with detaching soles that flapped when I walked, provided humiliations of my own. I remember especially my winter coat, the ends of the sleeves with the worn-away threads hanging loose, like two straggly beards dangling down from my wrists.

I had one short-lived hope for rescue from this particular shame. In the fourth grade I had begun to write what it pleased me to call "poems"—doggerel of rhymed couplets that I'd scribble on whatever scraps of paper I could get my hands on. More than several times I'd come up with what's now called an "occasional" poem. Here's a sample from my mother's Mother's Day tribute: "When in disaster/No one could get there any faster." All evidence to the contrary, I had not yet become acquainted with the work of Ogden Nash.

But this was my hope: There were two middle-aged women of our acquaintance who, for reasons all their own, found me entertaining, and I would recite my poems for them. Their response was all that could have been desired. They were amazed at the depth and breadth of my gift. They had also, on one occasion, commented on the decorative nature of my coat sleeves. An idea was instantaneous: I would copy out all my poems, make of them an approximation of a book, present it to the (to me) affluent ladies, and they would buy me a new coat.

I copied out the poems. I put them together with yarn threaded through holes made by a paring knife. I gave them to the ladies. Great cries of praise. Repeated expressions of gratitude. The visit progressed. I was, as always, entertaining. They were pleased. They had a good time. The visit ended, as did my expectation.

Less than three weeks into my therapy a phone call came just after I got home from work. My older sister, Helen Margaret, said, "Franny died." Franny was my younger sister, the last of my parents' eight children. A suicide at the age of twenty-eight, the divorced mother of three children (ages nine to five). Pills. Franny was found on her kitchen floor that morning by our sister

Sally. Franny's third attempt, each more determined than the last. Institutionalized for a time after the second.

I had visited her there. I made a trip to Wisconsin for that express purpose, a rare event. I did visit the family from time to time; sometimes more than a few years passed between trips. Financial considerations to some degree, but even more, a reluctance to descend into the maelstrom that had gathered at the depth of my family's life.

It was Franny's situation. Court-approved rescue from a disastrous marriage, with no financial support from her ex-husband, and three children in need of a structured life, understandably hungry for attention and affection. These needs were present in even greater measure in Franny herself, intensified no doubt by the absence of sexual fulfillment and the loving help of a supportive mate, which her husband definitely had not been. (For their honeymoon, according to my mother, Franny was taken—already pregnant—to Chicago, deposited in a hotel room and left pretty much to herself for the weeklong adjustment to married life.)

It was a problem with no solution. As a Catholic, she could not marry again, even if she'd wanted to, without renouncing a strong familial allegiance to the Catholic Church. The apparatus for an annulment, in the intervening years between the divorce and the suicide, was in the hands of a Jesuit at Gesu Church in Milwaukee who was presumably her advocate. He interviewed me and I gave him what I am certain were the proofs needed to justify an annulment.

Jim, the husband, had been a friend of mine; we'd met when we worked together at Walgreen's, I as a soda jerk, he as a clerk on what was referred to as "the drug side," where prescriptions were filled and clerks sold over-the-counter medicines and all the other products shelved in drugstores at the time: cosmetics, candy, cigarettes, Kleenex, etc. Our most prominent activity together was ice skating, mostly at Washington Park, where the boating lagoon froze over each and every winter. From time to time he came over to my house. He met my family.

One evening when he was there, sitting on the couch, Franny brought him a cup of steaming tea. She knelt in front of him and held it up as if it were an offering. She looked directly into his eyes. He looked directly into hers. What followed needs no elaboration.

At this same time the Cold War was intensifying and there were calls for bringing back the draft. I didn't want to be drafted into the army so I voluntarily enlisted in the Air Force. Franny and Jim became engaged. I was to be the best man at the elaborate church wedding.

The night before, possibly to make sure Jim would show up the next morning, I stayed at his place. His unreliability when it came to honoring dates to arriving at the agreed-upon hour, or coming at all, was well established. Possibly, because Franny was already pregnant (unknown to any of the family), she ignored or accepted these "idiosyncrasies" and went ahead with the marriage. More likely, however, was that she was passionately and helplessly attached to Jim and willing to endure whatever might be necessary to secure and make permanent the promised bond.

During the evening of the night I spent at his house, he, without any prompting or questioning on my part, acknowledged that his conversion to Catholicism and his agreement to a Catholic ceremony had no meaning for him. He believed none of it; he accepted none of it. This was all said casually, without the least note of scorn. He was not admitting to any hypocrisy or deception. Whether this alone would invalidate the marriage according to the Church's Canon Law, I do not know, but as part of the larger pattern of Jim's inability or refusal to make and honor a commitment, this surely deserves consideration. Then, too, there was Franny's decision to tell no one about the pregnancy. Fear? Shame? That she had isolated herself so completely from our mother and our sisters does more than merely suggest an emotional state that disqualified her from making and implementing the most important decision of her life.

The known truths are beyond contradiction, sufficient evidence not to just make the marriage eligible for annulment but to require that the judgment be expedited and Franny made free to marry without the threat of sacramental refusal or diminished status in the Catholic community. Whether there were additional reasons supportive of her cause, I do not know. What I do know is that either clerical indifference, bureaucratic sloth, hierarchical opposition, or whatever other power involved delay to the point of criminality, a promulgation was never made.

This is not an idle accusation. In effect, Franny was condemned to a life of loneliness with no hope of a fulfilled love, but she was also forbidden to even go in search of such a possibility. How contributory this was to her suicide, no one can truly know, since the complexities of her nature—of anyone's—can never be untangled and expertly woven into a meaningful pattern. But surely these were needless and monstrous burdens added to those she was already being forced to bear. Her children, fortunately, were adopted by Helen Margaret and her Brooklyn-born husband, Tom Smith, who lovingly raised and nurtured them. The tragedy, however, must always have been for them, as for all of us, a hovering presence that could never be completely exorcised.

What I experienced when I came back to New York after Franny's funeral was predictable. I went through the motions of living. I went to work. I went to Dr. Gould. I said my prayers—ostensibly for Franny, and I think they were—but on occasion I couldn't be sure that my *De profundis* didn't include an unarticulated plea that Gale and I would be together again, that I could lie down by his side and be comforted. The fervor of my plea was determined by the hopelessness of my cause. For Franny, however, my prayer was closer to a demand than a petition. In no way would I accept that my sister, in her suffering, could be judged guilty of the claim that a suicide was beyond the reach of God's love and of God's mercy. Can one suffer what Franny had suffered and then be *punished?*

6.

I had finally finished the play I was working on while volunteering for *The Catholic Worker*. It was called *Seen from a Cockeyed Kite*, inspired by an anecdote told to me by a Yale undergraduate, Brandon Stoddard, who'd performed in a play of mine produced by the Drama School. He'd gone to a prestigious prep school, Deerfield Academy, in Massachusetts. In his class was a boy, Johnny Gunther, who, in their senior year, was diagnosed with an incurable brain tumor. There were treatments and surgeries. Johnny wanted desperately, Brandon told me, to experience some meaningful achievement before his death. He became determined to graduate. And graduate he did; his head bandaged, his step faltering as he mounted the stage and was awarded his diploma.

I was very moved. To be so young, to be confronted

so brutally by mortality, the confusion, the yearnings left unfulfilled, all deeds not done. I would write a play, not about Brandon's friend—Johnny's father, John Gunther, had already done that in a book knowingly titled, *Death Be Not Proud*, but my play would be informed by my own searchings into this kind of tragedy, a boy's determination to experience a defining achievement before a predicted death.

The play was performed Off-Broadway at the Actor's Playhouse on Seventh Avenue. It opened on September 13, 1961. I was convinced it would secure for me the inevitable fame and fortune that I'd predicted for myself. After the first-night performance, I was briefly interviewed by a woman who would report on the play along with my comments on her radio show: "You, Joseph Caldwell," she intoned, "have written an American classic in the tradition of *Our Town* and *The Glass Menagerie*." Since this was hardly news to me, I accepted her kind words with equanimity. The other more powerful critics were not so kind. "If we have to have a play like this this season," one critic wrote, "how fortunate we've had it now and it's behind us and we can get on with the rest of the season." So much for my prediction.

A week after the closing of my flop play, I made the destined move from Hague Street. (I gave the Franklin stove to Gale. He thanked me.) The move itself coincided perfectly with a similarly drastic change in my identity. For those nine years on Hague Street, I had been deemed "a promising playwright"——a designation substantiated by the aforementioned Arts of the Theatre Foundation Award, my two fellowships, and a major production at Yale. I was also an active member of New Dramatists and was included in the playwright's unit of the prestigious Actors Studio, which allowed me to sit in on the acting sessions (and gave me a quick glimpse of "Marilyn" wearing no makeup and with a small kerchief on her head. She looked like the flawlessly fresh-faced girl next door).

Now I was a "failed playwright," holding no promise whatsoever. It was more than a matter of being sent back to "GO" from where I'd just begin all over again. I was now stigmatized with that most dreaded word in a writer's vocabulary: "failure." All that had gone before was nullified, and it was only right that I should be evicted from the premises in which I'd lived with such encouraging expectations. What I had been I no longer was and should without ceremony be removed from the enviable precincts of youthful possibility.

That the play flopped proved in time to be a well-disguised blessing. Had it succeeded, I would have felt that my preference to be noted as a playwright of "sensibility" had been validated and I would continue to present myself as someone sensitive and unthreatening, incapable of aggression or cynicism. In other words, as something I was not, which, as I would learn, could be fatal to a writer. My true work would not be possible until I could admit to myself that I was who I was: angry, competitive, and all those other adjectives that I had thought might justify rejection. To ward off that feared rejection, I rejected myself. What I was to be afflicted with now was inevitable: writer's block.

There are probably as many causes for this condition as there are writers—and just as many solutions. Since I'm familiar with only my own, I'll stick with them and avoid any generalizations. I've already identified the source—self-censorship—which, in turn, prompted my imagination (my most vital asset) to shut itself down. Because of its innate integrity it refused to be complicit in a lie.

This had become only too apparent in the play I next tried to write, *The Downtown Holy Lady*. The seed for this had been planted during a talk by Eammon Hennacy I attended at *The Catholic Worker* sometime after my earlier association. It was on the second floor of the loft building on Spring Street, close to the heart of Little Italy. I'd noticed that the front windows had been covered with heavy plastic sheeting—and I soon discovered the reason that it had been put in place.

Not long after the talk had begun, several large rocks, one after the other, came crashing through the window. Without pause, Eammon glanced over his right shoulder and said, "The Catholics are throwing stones at us again."

The "Catholics," of course, were the Italian neighbors who deeply resented having a food line and a "house of hospitality" on one of their streets. This, in a way, was greatly different from Little Italy's response to the first years of *The Worker*. It was on Mott Street in the heart—both literally and figuratively—of Little Italy. Those years, however, were in the depth of the Great Depression and the food line had extended on some occasions down the block and down part of the next. The neighbors were welcoming and even proud of what was being offered.

Of course, the circumstances then were radically different. Those in the line then were the desperate unemployed—a constituency readily recognizable as some of their own. In the late fifties, during a period of shared prosperity, the food line was peopled primarily by derelicts congregating around the flophouses and bars on the Bowery, very definitely a blight on Little Italy's thriving community. Operative here was the ineradicable distinction between the so-called deserving poor, and the so-called undeserving poor. In a way, the hostility can hardly be surprising.

A seed began to stir in my imagination. What I got, for starters, was the idea of an aging priest, eager to leave behind some legacy to climax his years of service. He would install in front of his church a statue of its patron, Michael the Archangel, his wings outspread, his sword unsheathed. To raise money there would be a parade through the streets.

And here's where the play would begin. A woman with a small deli–sized restaurant has given a free meal to a shabbily dressed bag woman who left her shopping bag behind. The bag happens to be stuffed with money. To lure the woman back to collect her bag, she begins to feed more and more of those in need. The neighbors object.

So I had my situation: a clash between the old pieties for statues and candles and the central mission of Christianity of caring for those in need. All I had to do was dramatize the process by which these forces resolve, or fail to resolve, themselves.

As heaven would have it, Yale was offering six playwriting fellowships for the coming academic year, part of a workshop that would also include six third-year Drama School playwriting students. If I were accepted, it would be my third Yale fellowship.

I applied by sending in a paperback version of *Cock-eyed Kite*, which had been published at his own expense by a young enthusiast who found in it qualities that had escaped the critics. I guess he had good instincts because on the basis of it I got in. I told myself, writer's block or not, that with this opportunity everything would change. My work would flourish and I would become again a laudable writer.

Such was not to be the case. To begin with, when I'd phoned my former mentor from those years before and told him I'd been chosen, he made the mistake of telling me that he was particularly pleased because the last he'd heard was that I was first alternate. One of the original six had apparently dropped out. I was the least of the chosen six. In my battered psychic state, this was not helpful knowledge.

What I'd gotten myself into was two semesters to be devoted entirely to the writing of the play I was expected to write.

It was one of the more wretched periods of my life. My imagination would not be goaded into action. It still refused to open wide a store of revelations and insights in answer to my pleadings. It refused to give me the inspired scenes that only I could write.

Painfully, despairingly, I struggled on. I wrote—and then I wrote some more. But this was not the way writing should be. For each of my previous plays I'd realized that a "work in progress" was a continuing series of revelations, gifts served up by a fertile imagination. With that most needed tool denied me, I had to resort to my intellect—for me, a far from sufficient solution. (For obvious reasons, I had earlier been relieved to realize that my intellect was not my primary instrument. Compared to my brothers and sisters, I'm the family dumb bunny.)

Even under my present circumstance, I still had two faithful attributes that had not deserted me: my craftsmanship and a fairly good ear for dialogue. But without revelations, I had to come up with ideas—ideas for scenes that would advance the plot, then struggle to summon some way to make them interesting. I would take long walks, most often to East Rock, where I'd climb the switchback steps to the top of the cliff to see all of Yale, all of New Haven, spread out before me. And all of my memories from seven years before when I would have reveled without challenge to the life then being made available: eager creativity, rewarding achievement.

Added to all this, New Haven in those intervening years had lost all its elm trees to the continental blight. Street after street after street that had been of uncommon beauty were now denuded thoroughfares offering nothing more than a minimal convenience in getting from here to there. It didn't occur to me at the time to see this as an accurate metaphor for my own diminished condition, so I'll just let it remain simply itself, one more absence from among the splendors I'd previously known.

The play progressed. My colleagues and the workshop's mentor, David Davidson, were for the most part encouraging about the work I was doing, and I kept my disappointments to myself.

As the end of our time together approached, David took me to the most expensive restaurant in New Haven—not Casey's but one reputed to be even more expensive. His purpose, he admitted, was to ask me if I had been aware that I was the first alternate for one of the fellowships.

"No," I lied, because it was simpler than going into what I considered a painful subject. He then went on to note that I had been accepted last but had proved to be the most gifted. This was, of course, ironically welcome, but the satisfaction had its limits. I was, after all, nearing the end of one of the more difficult years I'd ever lived through.

Ultimately the resources that hadn't given up on me—my craftsmanship and my ear for dialogue—had responded rather generously, and my play and a play by another of the fellows were being considered for the final major production of the year. For me this would have been a repeat of a previous honor. The other play was chosen and, to be honest, I was not all that disappointed. I didn't feel my work was completed. I hadn't been able to give it all that it deserved, all that it needed.

If that were the end of this sorry tale, I'd be content. But what I did next was nothing short of shameful. I betrayed my play. Instead of continuing the struggle to give it its fulfillment, I reworked it into something I thought might be more marketable. I had never let this be a consideration before—nor have I since.

Although it in no way excuses my decision, I note here that if the theater is to secure its vitality, it must change (as the times change, as audiences change). And the changes were, for me, formidable. I've already mentioned the dismissal of the "play of sensibility," but what had overwhelmed and replaced it were highly uncongenial to a playwright reluctant to deal with the less attractive aspects of his nature.

First there was the Theater of the Absurd, which challenged my need to bring order out of chaos (Ionesco, Beckett). Then, too, plays dramatizing cynical hostility (Albee the avatar).

My *Downtown Holy Lady* was permitted to retain only its title. The rest was garbage. The conflict was now between a woman and her adulterous boyfriend. She was feeding the poor; he was afraid of the competition. When it was given the inadequate production it deserved, Off-Off-Broadway, my matronly cousin from Connecticut who had seen my three previous plays provided the definitive critique. "That is the worst thing you're ever going to write." I have tried since to prove her correct.

During all this time I'd still been seeing Dr. Gould, going to New York from New Haven once a week for a one-on-one session with him as well as a group session. I was beginning, not without difficulty, to know myself better and, with even more difficulty, accepting what I was discovering.

It's here that I reduce my terrifying panic attacks to a mere footnote.

Working my way through the labyrinth of my mind with Dr. Gould, I came to realize that the cause was deeply repressed anger. I was writing, during some of this time, the commentary for WQXR. One of my colleagues went on vacation as did the head of our unit. I took on some of the vacationer's assignments, expecting another writer to do the same. He refused repeatedly to be the least bit of help. I took on all of the work. No insistence on fair play. Goody-Two-Shoes Caldwell took it all onto himself, working his butt off. Without the least whimper of complaint, completely denying the wrath that would reveal my truer nature. Deeper down in my psyche I raged against myself. Why hadn't I stood up for myself? Why hadn't I asserted myself? I was complicit in the injustice. All this compressed anger threatened to explode, spattering my detonated brain against the stones of the Brooklyn Bridge.

My reluctance to show aggression was what lay at the source of my writer's block. I had punitively silenced the one voice that could have spoken the truth. It took me a year to liberate my voice. One day, I made a direct, furious attack, not on the WQXR colleague who deserved it but on my dear, long-time friend Eddy Parone.

He and I were walking up Seventh Avenue in the Village after dinner together. Eddy, at the time, was enjoying a deserved reputation as one of the better directors of new and interesting Off-Broadway theater. We ran into a playwright, Leonard Melfi, who was a growing theater presence. Eddy told Leonard he was putting together an evening of short plays—about eight or ten minutes each—and would he please write one for him? The playwright casually agreed, and Eddy and I walked on.

During our entire evening together he had never mentioned the project, which would later have an Off-Broadway success titled *Collision Course*. As close a friend as I might be, he had written me off as a playwright. I was hurt. I was angry. But I said nothing.

The next morning I was bitterly determined to write a short play. I went into my living room. I reminded myself of what Chekhov was reputed to have said to a friend: "I can write a story about anything. See that ashtray? Do you want me to write a story about an ashtray?" (How unfair that there should be only one Chekhov.)

I looked around the room. I saw my rocking chair. I would write a play about a rocking chair. And, lo and behold, revelations that could come only from my imagination began to present themselves. Pounding away at my typewriter was my way of saying, "Take that, Eddy! See? I'm writing. I'm writing a real play. A real play, you son of a bitch."

In less than an hour I was finished. I phoned Eddy and told him I was coming over with a play for his project. I went over. He read it. He crossed out half of the last page. He'd let me know. But I already knew.

Soon after, he told me it wasn't right for what he had in mind. But nothing could diminish my satisfaction. Maybe Eddy didn't know it. But I did. I was a playwright again.

The first full-length play I wrote after my true identity as a playwright had been restored was actually a rewrite. In a way I was indeed going back to "GO," to where I'd originally started. The rewritten play, titled *The King and Queen of Glory*, was, in its beginnings, the first of my writings for which I was paid—in this instance, in 1954, an hourlong television drama, titled at that time, *Giant Killer* and aired on NBC.

This play and the television script are the closest I've ever come to autobiography. It's my response to my father's devastation when the firstborn child of his late-in-life marriage, my eldest sister, Mary Ellen, entered a religious order, the Sisters of Charity of the Blessed Virgin Mary, the summer after her high-school graduation.

In those days, when a girl age seventeen entered a convent, she removed herself almost completely from her family. Her life was now dedicated to the rigors and demands of religious life. My father was losing his most beloved child. He would also, the following year, be retiring from his lifelong job. My oldest brother, Jim, speculated that our father believed that Mary Ellen was joining the Order because it was the only possible way she would get the education her superior intelligence deserved. My father had failed her. If that's what he thought, he was very much in the wrong. Her calling was genuine, and she gave almost eighty years of rewarding service.

At one time she was head of the Theology Department at her Order's Clarke College in Iowa. Because she was a tenured professor, a college in a secular situation would have provided a tuition-free education for her children. To compensate for this impossibility, nieces and nephews were eligible in their stead. My sister, with her vow of poverty, put one niece and three nephews through college.

The plot of the play revolves around whether the teenage girl can conscientiously leave her family when it will soon be without a sufficient income after the father's retirement. All this sort of works its way out, not the way it really happened, but I intended the play to be a tribute to my father—and tributes, by their nature, often allow for revision if basic truths are respected. And the basic truth here was that my father suffered—and attention must be paid.

It gives me a particular satisfaction that this was the subject to which I returned when a return was finally made possible.

I cannot leave my writings about my father with only the few sentences already included. Allow me to offer the following:

I have written of my father's near two-year alcoholic binge as his response to his humiliation as an inadequate provider for his family. To give some redemptive balance to this record, here is an anecdote that is more expressive of my father's deeper nature. To begin, I note that he not only survived his binge, but found rewarding employment as the head of the mailing and messenger unit of a thriving factory in Milwaukee and died in his sleep at age 74 after working a full schedule the day before.

Here's the anecdote. My father didn't like dogs. He probably had some unfortunate experience in his early years that caused his lifelong antipathy. My sister Franny and I pleaded again and again to be allowed to have a puppy. He finally relented—with the provision that it wouldn't be a female.

Franny heard of a litter of four pups in the neighborhood, but when she went to make her claim, only a female puppy was left. With little effort, we decided to lie. We informed my father that the puppy was a male. We brought her home. We named her Nick. Fortunately, my father's dislike was limited to indifference and he never bothered to verify the dog's gender.

When fully grown, Nick was a little over sixteen inches tall to the tip of her ears. She had a full complement of white fur and was an eager playmate. Only once was she unhappy. Franny and I dressed her in a T-shirt and tied a red bandanna around her neck. She hung her head in shame at having her doggyhood so foolishly desecrated. The T-shirt and the bandanna came off; we all immediately reverted to our shared energetic enjoyments.

We trained her not only to sit, but to accept on the tip of her snout a piece of something to eat—usually a slice of salami—and to listen to our stern command that she not eat it. After a few seconds of obedience, we, with a quick snap of our fingers, would shout triumphantly, "Okay!" and, with a quick flick of her snout she would take the salami into her mouth and down her gullet it to our repeated cries of joy. The praise and the petting that followed, with Nick's paws pressed into Franny's thighs, her tail and tongue wagging, almost overwhelmed the three of us. Only a disciplined restraint kept Franny and me from repeating the trick again and again until the family's supply of salami was completely depleted.

Two years into our continuing joy—I was about fourteen by then—my mother came running up the stairs early one morning, calling out, "Joe! Get up! Nick's had pups!" As she raced back down the steps, I shouted, "How did that happen?" Without pause, she answered, "Only one way it could have happened!" One of my mother's few direct references to sex.

Downstairs, under the protection of the kitchen table, there was Nick, our playmate, stretched out, patiently nursing four fist-sized puppies that had yet to open their eyes. She'd somehow appropriated a sweater, a scarf, and a dish towel, and had fashioned a rather comfortable bed on which to give birth and care for her offspring.

The moment of truth for my father came after I'd gone off to serve as altar boy for eight o'clock Mass. My mother gave me a full report when I came home for lunch. The wrath for which we'd all prepared ourselves, the infuriated accusations of deceit, the thundering threats of reprisal, had failed to find expression. Apparently, my father, a man who had sired eight children, when confronted with our perfidy could see only a mother lovingly tending her newborn babies. It was all over from that moment on. No one in our household would be more concerned that Nick was getting what Nick needed, what Nick wanted, than my father. "Does Nick want to go out?" "Does Nick have enough water?" And so on and on. This, too, was my father.

I ran into Gale not long after the brief run of my flopped *Cock-eyed Kite*. He was taking the A train uptown from the Village. He'd seen the play. He liked it. The train arrived. There was time for me to plant my right hand firmly on his back and thank him. Then he stepped into the train, the doors closed, and the train sped on its way.

It rattled me to see him. And it would rattle me again. The phrase "to go weak in the knees" is more than an overused description dramatizing an unexpected encounter. It's an accurate physical description of what would overwhelm me at the sight of him. It happened again at the Museum of Modern Art when we both ended up in a throng of enthusiasts who had come to see the Turner paintings. Then I saw him again at St. Marks Bookshop on Eighth Street, where he informed me that his name was no longer Gale. It was Bill, which was a diminutive of William, his actual first name. (For that reason, I will call him Bill from now on.) He'd grown a bushy beard and let his hair grow to near hippie length.

At a later date I saw him at the Metropolitan Museum commenting in a very authoritative but easygoing manner on the paintings included in a major showing of Van Gogh at Arles. I wasn't close enough to hear what he was saying, but I noticed that the beard had been trimmed and he was dressed a bit more respectably than usual—a jacket—but at least he'd decided against a tie—which I had never seen him wear.

As usual, I was undone and my knees reverted to the near-useless state that was their assigned response to his sudden appearance. Rather than go up to him and say hello, I positioned myself in front of a painting next to the one he was commenting on. I would let him see me first and oblige him to make the initial greeting. I stood there. He turned his attention to the painting where I was standing, but took no notice of me. Before my agitation could get worse, I realized that this wasn't Bill after all, but a near enough replica that made it possible for me to call it an honest mistake. Still, I was unable to reclaim my previous concentration. My equilibrium, both emotional and physical, had been so thoroughly unsettled that I was unable to summon the undivided attention the rest of the show demanded. I left.

I walked past one magnificent work of art after another, taking no notice whatsoever. Foolish, of course. Tell that to my knees.

It wasn't nearly that bad when we would get together by common consent. I was fully aware by the late sixties, early seventies that a reconciliation—or whatever you want to call it—was never to be and it would be inadvisable for me to press my cause, persistent though the impulse might be.

One evening, while I was still living on the Lower East Side, Bill came to dinner. We had a good time. After dinner, he was stretched out on my living room couch very much enjoying the plot of a play he was telling me I should write. It was a parody of a farm girl

coming to New York, living wildly among stereotypi-
cally unsavory characters, and coming not to a bad but
a good end where she is rich and celebrated.

He was being goofy. The plot wasn't all that imaginative, and he was trying a little too hard. But I had
no difficulty pretending to appreciate his presumed
inventiveness. It began to occur to me that he would
perhaps be more than willing to stay the night. Instead
of thrilled expectation, it came into my mind that this
would have to be *his* choice. I thought of all the many
times I had needed to be with him, but knew it was
impossible. I resented that *his* preference would prevail
now whereas mine had been consistently dismissed.
Perversely, I decided I would not ask him to spend the
night. And I didn't.

Even as I saw him to the door, I could tell that this
was not what he'd intended, but I was showing so little
interest in anything intimate that he declined to make
any move or say anything that would change the direction the evening had taken. He left.

I went to bed. I went to sleep. Toward morning I
was awakened by a nearby voice. I was not talking to
myself. Nor was I dreaming. The voice very distinct-
ly said, "You fool! Do you think you're going to live
forever?" The meaning was: "When will this chance
come again?" It would be close to fifteen years before
we would see each other again.

7.

During part of this middle period, I experienced a somewhat radical change in my writing career. I began working on the television soap operas *Love of Life*, *Secret Storm*, and *Dark Shadows*. In no way was I dismissive of the genre, nor did I arrogantly feel I was debasing myself by lending my name to its obvious appropriation of melodrama and sentimentality. Quite to the contrary. My involvement gave me a certain respect for its achievements.

True, the characters were unfailingly inflicted with challenges that would threaten their survival or their happiness. At one point it even occurred to me that some enterprising student might, for a thesis, examine the eager sadism at the core of the soaps. (Example: When I was writing *Love of Life*, Bruce, a sympathetic character, had become a paraplegic because of a blow to his head when confronting a serial killer. One day, when I arrived at the apartment of the show's head writer, who did the plotting, he gleefully welcomed me with the words "They drop Bruce.")

What a putative doctoral thesis could not ignore, however, was the inspiration at the source of this devastation. Bruce and his loved ones, his wife, his son, his friends, would gallantly rise to the occasion and eventually triumph. This, I never doubted, explained the lure of the soaps, the affirmation of human tenacity, the power of love and caring. The soaps, to my thinking, responded to a basic need, the assurance that, eventually, all would, in the words of Oscar Wilde in his definition of fiction, end happily for the good people and unhappily for the bad people. And while doing all this—possibly most important of all—they would tell a good story.

When writing my first show, *Love of Life*, however, I realized once again that I was full of rage, rage that my freedom had been taken from me, my freedom to write what I wanted to write the way I wanted to write it. Except that this freedom had *not* been taken from me. I had voluntarily handed it over; my anger should have been directed toward myself. But such are the convenient complexities of human conduct. I was able, with no pause for such a consideration, to blame the head writer, Don. He would give me a one- or two-paragraph outline of a scene, setting out what the action would be and how the plot would be advanced. It was then my job to invent the activities and write the dialogue for the characters—all of which must please Don. There were times when he would rewrite what I'd written. No one rewrites what I write unless I agree. Without exaggerating, I can honestly say that there were times when I'd have to decide whether to murder Don or to write the script. Fortunately for both of us, I chose to write the script.

And yet I could not be unaware of the devoted allegiance of the viewers, their intimate involvement with the characters. It was not unknown for a viewer to write a letter not to the actor but to the character, warning: "Watch out for Kaye. She doesn't mean a word of what she says." "Your husband is being unfaithful with the woman next door." Or a hope for a greater intimacy. "If you and your mother—'the characters'—ever come to California, you can stay with us."

I myself was once given the privilege of being directly involved in a viewer's intense experience of *Love of Life*. Don was a master of plotting. One of his more surefire plots was inspired by Joan Copeland, a superior but underutilized actress of her generation. As a privileged member of the Playwrights' Unit at the Actors Studio, I had watched as she did a scene from a well-received play of the time: *The Girl on the Via Flaminia*. She was superb, unforgettably so.

But Lee Strasberg, the head of the studio (and the biggest windbag in history), appraised her work at length, careful not to include the least word of encouragement. He kept his charges in thrall by the simple expedient of withholding approval, that response actors live for.

Miss Copeland had, on *Love of Life*, played a dying wife and mother who had used her final months to find for her husband and daughter a successor who would give them both the love and the comfort they would desperately need after her death. She chose a warm-hearted but sophisticated woman named Tammy who has chosen the small-town life as opposed to her previous Broadway stardom to help her successful recovery from alcoholism. After a shameless succession of farewell scenes between wife and husband, as well as mother and daughter, the wife went to her reward and Tammy was there to be with them in their bereavement. This led to a romance between Tammy and the husband, just as the saintly wife had planned.

Don apologized not at all that the idea came from a movie, *No Sad Songs for Me*. When an acquaintance once asked him, "Did you ever see a movie called *No Sad Songs for Me*? Don had ready the perfect answer. "Was that a musical?"

So successful and popular had Miss Copeland been on the show that Don decided to bring her back as her character's evil sister. She was given a blond wig and the name "Kaye." She turned up at the home of her brother-in-law, Link, and his teenage daughter, Sandy. She would woo them both, marry into the somewhat affluent family, and set herself up for life. Again, Miss Copeland was magnificent and gave me my moment.

I was on the subway, on my way to a meeting with Don, going over the script I was about to give him. A tug on my left sleeve. I turned to the woman next to me. Without preamble, she fervently said, "Oh, I hope Link doesn't marry Kaye!" I held up my right hand as if taking an oath. "He won't. I promise you." No more words were spoken between us.

As something of a sequel to this, Don was plotting the return of Tammy to her career as a Broadway star. Because of Kaye and her determination to win Link, Tammy's love life was in shambles. *However*, lo and behold, a Broadway producer who was an old friend sent her the manuscript of a play by a young playwright who had died but whose mother was determined that the world know of her son's extraordinary gifts.

Tammy had sworn off her acting career but, in her present circumstance, she might be susceptible to persuasion.

During one of my Monday meetings with Don to discuss the new set of outlines, Don said, "I'm going to go get a haircut. While I'm out I want you to write that great speech we talked about that would end the play." It would be spoken by Tammy as the pioneer farm woman to her dead son held across her knees as in a *pietà*. This must be the speech that would persuade Tammy to take on the part and set in motion her dramatic return to Broadway as a reigning star.

Don left. I thought for a few minutes, then wrote the speech. It began, "I have slaughtered the stallion and the mare." She goes on to tell of the near-demented devastation she has wrought upon all her land, her response to the betrayed love that had been the substance of the play. Her last words to her dead son are "Rest now. And wait for me."

Don came back, his hair shorn. He read it. With a somewhat surprised shrug, he said, "It's a great speech."

Tammy took the part, and many were the times the speech was repeated during the soap opera play's rehearsals and, of course, on the play's tumultuous opening night.

Months later, at a party, a young man who easily anticipated the hippie movement that lay in the not-too-distant future—untamed hair, "distressed" clothing, an indifference to hygiene (and sexy in the extreme)—recited for me, word perfect, the entire speech. I never saw him again.

At another point a friend of mine who was watching the show asked, "What kind of play is it?" Rather loftily, I said, "It's a Eugene O'Neill play written by García Lorca," thereby inadvertently giving a measure to my writing ambitions as well as to the sad distance between my aspirations and my achievements.

Another advantage of soap-opera writing was the opportunity to be shameless. Utterly and completely shameless. For *Secret Storm* I was one of a team of co-writers. We did the plotting together.

In one sequence, there was a sympathetic character named Kitty, a single mother, who struggled to care for her little boy aged about four. An evil man who'd been spurned by Kitty brings made-up facts before the civil authorities, who declare Kitty to be an unfit mother. Her little boy will be taken from her. When did that happen? My doing: on Christmas Eve, of course. Decorated tree. Presents. He's taken away.

Wait, there's more. Kitty, alone, hears voices outside singing Christmas carols. Enraged, she flings open the door. There, two waif-like urchins are piping away in their child voices. She invites them in and gives them all the presents. How shameless could I get? Now you know.

On to *Dark Shadows*. When I taught at Columbia and NYU and at the 92nd Street Y, more than several times at the first session I would be asked by one of my students, "Are you the Joe Caldwell who wrote *Dark Shadows*? I would confess. My authority immediately went up a notch.

A team of three writers would plot the show in the presence of the producer, Dan Curtis. These were extended, agonizing meetings during which Dan would practice putting golf balls. After one long session, he mentioned as something of an afterthought, "I want a vampire for the kids for the summer."

One of the other writers, Ron Sproat, and I left, headed for a gay bar on West 23rd Street to have a drink and commiserate. What's a vampire but a serial killer? You track him down, drive a stake through his heart, and move on to the next bright idea.

By the time Ron and I got to either our second

or third drink (dry bourbon Manhattans with George Dickel bourbon—the name was irresistible), we had decided to give the serial killer a singular idiosyncrasy that would invest the character with an emotional life, which would in turn give us something to write about. We would make him a *reluctant* vampire. Forever he would mourn his expulsion from the human family.

The bloodlust that nourished him and gave him immortality brought him more shame than satisfaction. His only restriction was that he must finish his nocturnal predations and be safely stretched out in his coffin before the sun came up. As you can see, the opportunities for imaginative tribulations that lie at the heart of the soap-opera genre made the writing at times quite enjoyable, especially if you consider that the vampiric identity as an outcast, whether a viewer realized it or not, was familiar to Ron and to me as gay men—the exclusion from the human family, the prohibited fulfillment of shared love, etc. Central to the vampire were yearnings that made him vulnerable and even sympathetic. Ron and I shared with him those vulnerabilities.

Thanks to our Dickel decision, the show took off. The number of viewers, most of them teenagers, reached its peak: *Dark Shadows* became a cult classic. Little did they suspect why, but it's really quite obvious. The show was all about compulsive sex. Name the teenager, including oneself, who didn't, in near-vampiric desperation, feel at one time or another, "I've got to have it or I'll die!"

It is with a particular glee that I savor the realization that Dan Curtis, a committed homophobe, had his greatest success with his most famous character, Barnabas Collins, a vampire, a man knowingly created by two gay men, who in their own way were dramatizing their own plight.

For fear of homoeroticism in the show, Dan decreed that the vampire could bite a woman on the neck but bite a man only on his wrist. But there was an even more explicit demonstration of his homophobia. During one of our plotting sessions, Dan lowered his tone to emphasize the gravity of what he was about to say: "I heard that Louie Edmonds [who played Roger Collins] is queer. Do I have to fire him?"

He had chosen his advisers wisely. Had we ruled against Louie, Dan, to be consistent, would have had to divest himself of two-thirds of his writing staff, as well as the actor playing the vampire and another actor, who played a dashing romantic lead. A valued actress could also have been given the axe. Ron and I, however, managed, with straight (unavoidable pun) faces, to assure our producer that Louie was a good actor, that a replacement would confuse the viewers, and that he in no way imperiled the show. Dan submitted to our counsel and we all kept our jobs.

Sad to say, I had made that promise to myself when I started to write for the soaps that I would do it for no more than six months, then use the accumulated money to support my own work for the half year following, I kept the promise even though the show was headed for cult popularity. The real fun was just beginning. And I could have been involved with a vampire, a witch, a werewolf, and assorted periods of time and place. Not a good career move.

The show's enthusiasts persisted in their adulation even after the object of their fanaticism was no longer being produced. Their core connection to each other and the show was a regular mailing of the *Shadowgram*, edited by the devoted and indefatigable Marcy Robin. The continuing careers of the actors and the writers were recorded. Important incidents, celebrity appearances, even deaths were given their due. But the cult's most extravagant expression of their continuing allegiance was an annual festival, usually in a hotel convention center that could accommodate several hundred people. The votaries would congregate at these sites across the continent, some of them replicating a favorite character. The main attraction, however, was a presentation by one of the actors or writers, sharing inside information and recalling fond memories.

When one of the celebrations was in New Jersey, I was the invited speaker. I think I included along with other remarks the epiphanic moment experienced by Ron and me that resulted in Barnabas being a "reluctant vampire," forgoing, of course, the gay source of this inspired realization.

The most memorable moment for me, however, came during the question-and-answer period after I'd spoken my piece. A woman in a red dress, seated in the third row, shot up her hand. Her question: "Why is it that your scripts for *Dark Shadows* were so sensitive and so eloquent, and your novels are so disgusting?"

In a surprising moment of quick thinking, I respectfully told her that we were there to talk about *Dark Shadows*, not my other writings. I was rather proud of how I controlled what could have become a difficult situation. Now I realize that I should have been more flustered and less adroit. I should have engaged her objections to the fullest, discussing all the unsavory, shocking, and disgusting aspects of my novels, the sex and the violence. Few things can attract interest to one's books more than a full-throated condemnation. She would have given my novels an inadvertent endorsement that money can't buy. If only I hadn't been so fast on my feet! Too late now.

At a later time, when I somehow managed to become poor again, I took a job as a messenger in the Wall Street area. It wasn't all that bad. I liked the irony of rushing around, carrying stocks and bonds worth millions when I was a hapless pauper myself. I wasn't cooped up in an office. I was out in the fresh air and it was spring. Still, I really preferred to make a bit more money. I asked a friend of mine who was attached to a reasonably successful soap, *Ryan's Hope*, if he could arrange for me to write some trial scripts. This did not mean that I was going back on my resolve never to work for the soaps again. Those who wrote trial scripts were providing the show with a small number of writers who might prove their capabilities and at the same time become familiar with the show itself, ready if a replacement was needed. I would write six trial scripts, take the money, and run.

I wrote four. When I got that far, the head writer, who possibly was not privy to my plan, phoned me and told me I would be writing no more scripts. I quote her: "To write for *Ryan's Hope* you have to have a spiritual dimension [dementia?]. Either you have it, or you don't have it, and *you* don't have it." This was news to me, but I chose to be amused.

I simply thanked her, and with good reason. The show had provided me with close to four thousand dollars in fewer than four weeks.

But that fades into insignificance when, in my last script for the show, I had set down on paper for all time to come the most shameless line I've ever written, gallantry at its defiant best. The situation was this: A young cop had married a very young girl. His assignment now was to go on a sting operation against the Mafia and, to protect his wife, he had to get rid of her. (Don't ask me why. That's what the outline said: mine not to reason why.) The marriage had to be completely broken up and he was not allowed to even hint at the reason for this devastation so agonizing for them both. At the height of the scene, the cop says, "We should never have married in the first place! You're just a child! It was all wrong from the beginning! You're too young! You're just a child!"

To which she responds: "Your bride was a child. But your wife is a *woman!*"

When I'm asked, "Do you still write soap operas, I answer, "Not intentionally."

8.

It often seems that yearning is single-minded. It's nothing if not straightforward and unrelenting. But there are times when it invades actions and events to which it would seem to be completely unrelated, revealing itself only later to have been a presence during the first moments of the event's inception. Such was the case in 1963, when I realized that the Brooklyn Bridge had opened eighty years earlier on May 24, 1883.

This inspired me to throw a birthday party—on the bridge. On the raised footpath, with those stupendous views to be celebrated as well. I circulated invitations. I filled a gallon-sized thermos with vodka gimlets and got a gallon of Gallo burgundy. Paper party hats, noise-makers, streamers to be thrown and unfurled to welcome the guests—not only those invited but anyone and everyone passing by. (This preceded the bridge as the obligatory tourist attraction it has so deservedly become.)

Friends brought cheese and crackers, popcorn, and potato chips. The party quickly became overwhelmingly festive. Most welcome were those from distant lands who feared at first sight that they were being confronted by escaped inmates from a uniquely American madhouse. Soon enough we were all close to becoming friends for life. I got to tell tales about the building of the bridge, the genius and humanity of the Roeblings—John and Washington, father and son—and Washington's wife, Emily Warren Roebling. I even got to quote from Hart Crane's epic poem "The Bridge": "O harp and altar, of the fury fused."

We drank the Gallo and the gimlets. We ate the cheese and crackers, the chips, and the popcorn. We talked; we laughed; we celebrated. The dark was coming down. Merrily we cleared our mess, leaving not a chip behind. Singing as we went, we made the descent from the Roebling's immortal gift to us all.

My party had been a triumph. And then came the realization: I had wanted Bill to come out onto the bridge and find me there. This was a want well beyond hope and, even I, in the idiocy of my longing, did not for a moment allow my want to become an actual hope. I wasn't quite *that* crazy. But, I repeat, I had wanted it. And that want had been lurking unacknowledged through all the preparations, all the anxieties about the outcome. Would we be thrown off the bridge? Would we be arrested? All the accumulating thrills I'd made possible, the joy, the affection among the revelers, did not include Bill.

To be honest, I really did think on some subterranean level that I might, somehow, by some absurdly mystical emanation, have been able to make him appear—to materialize as if summoned by a beneficent power and become an approving participant of our rejoicings.

To give some measure to the success of the event, I, with minimal persuasion, agreed to repeat the celebration the next year and the year after that, and the year after that—which I did without being able to expunge completely my absurd longing.

This newly established tradition never failed to excite, and the invitations were a prized announcement, though all one had to do to be included was to walk out onto the bridge around six thirty on May 24 and be enthusiastically welcomed.

As the years passed, however, I finally reconciled myself to the simple fact that the prime purpose of my efforts would never come to pass: the sight of Gale coming toward me from the Brooklyn side.

After several years I stopped arranging and attending the event, but such was its hold on some of the regulars that they determined to continue without me. One impetus for the continuation was that my old friend Diffy had the same birthday as the bridge, and he had always been honored as an integral part of the celebration. I would continue to observe his birthday by simply joining him and several of the old friends for dinner afterwards. My friends indulged me and semi-accepted my intransigence about not attending.

Even after Diffy died, the determined celebrants persisted and I recently agreed to join them. Diffy's longtime companion, Yusube, had complained to me that two of the expected and cherished stalwarts, Cory and his wife Margie, would not be there. I knew he was experiencing an intensification of his loss of Diffy. How could I not have gone with him?

The party was well underway when Yusube and I made our way out to the middle of the footpath. There were possibly a dozen persisting partygoers, sharing the few bottles of wine they'd brought along. No hats, no noisemakers, no unfurled streamers to welcome us. Brownies, chips, cheese and a box of crackers were, however, available.

Some few remembered me and there were hugs. I was introduced to children from about three years old to some in their teens, all of them born since my defection. I drank some wine. I ate some cheese.

But what about Gale/Bill?

It is a central irony of yearning that, in its own way, absence can become a powerful presence. During all that I have written here about being on the bridge for a shabby replica of those other celebrations when I so ardently hoped he would appear, arriving from the Brooklyn side, his absence invaded every act of mine, every gesture, every word. For all my easy chatter, I was close to being overwhelmed by my unfulfilled longing. Gale's absence had, indeed, become that powerful presence.

I mentioned none of this to Yusube. Perhaps he in his grieving had experienced something similar.

He and I left before the sun had touched the horizon. We'd been there long enough. It was time to go.

9.

In those years during which I entertained on the bridge, I also began to write novels, starting with *In Such Dark Places*. I could never have even begun to write it had I not been given a residency at the Mac-Dowell Colony in New Hampshire. The book would be a coming-out novel, the main character a homosexual Catholic. Sound familiar? Though it would not be auto-biographical, it would be readily apparent that I didn't find the material under a cabbage. I wasn't sure I would have the courage to take it on. This was 1973. But my MacDowell acceptance meant to me that I was included in the continuum of writers who had been judged ca-pable of doing worthy work. With this, I was given the confidence to write what I really wanted to write.

I completed the novel three years later at Yaddo in Saratoga Springs, another retreat where a residency is, by definition, a vote of confidence, leading me to the realization that the ultimate contribution of places like Yaddo and MacDowell to the arts cannot be quantified. The volume of work is not the real measure of their importance. Nor is the number of prestigious awards won. It's the confidence they give to the artists that encourages them to take risks they would not have been able to take without this implicit validation. This may not be apparent to everyone, but it's true.

A Yaddo anecdote. Yaddo is a former country estate of hundreds of acres and four small lakes dominated by a fifty-five-room mansion with a grand staircase, Tiffany stained-glass windows, an intimidating great hall, an elaborate music room and a dining room.

My first dinner proved to be more than excruciating. I sat down at a table near the doorway to the great hall. The seat next to me was soon taken by a woman formidable to say the least: more hair than needed, large eyes, alert but welcoming. She held out her hand. "I'm Hortense Calisher." Famous, the wife of the director.

I said my name and we shook hands. "Good to meet you," I said. "But of course, I've been aware of your work going back to *The Catherine Wheel*." She smiled and said quietly, "*The Catherine Wheel* was written by Jean Stafford." So much for sucking up to the director's famous wife.

As for my novel, the main character would be a photographer. He would be a son of a bitch. About three sentences into the writing, it was revealed to me that he was not a son of a bitch. On the contrary, he was an honorable and confused young homosexual Catholic who ultimately realizes that the claims of charity take precedence over any misguided sense of unworthiness, a truth I had noted earlier, during my brief stint at *The Catholic Worker*.

The other main character is David, a fourteen-year-old urchin who lives by his wits, by occasional thievery, and is sexually agreeable to accommodating the teenage boys in the neighborhood who are either insatiable or insufficiently persuasive in their approach to teenage girls. The neighborhood in which it all takes place was to be around Tompkins Square. It would involve the parish of St. Brigid's.

The novel was published in 1978. About a year later, a very strange thing happened. I received a phone call: "May I speak to Joseph Caldwell?"

"This is he."

"This is John Cheever."

"Oh?"

"Are you interested in the Rome Prize?" This was the Rome Prize for literature awarded by the American Academy of Arts and Letters: a year in Rome to write.

Stunned, "Why yes, very much." To say the least.

"Well, you've got it."

Mr. Cheever then went on to tell me who had been on the jury of the American Academy that had made the award. (An imposing list I assure you. Cheever, Elizabeth Hardwick, and John Hollander, among others.) He told me I would come to the spring convocation of the Academy of Arts and Letters to receive the award, when I would go to Rome, and how much my stipend would be. It would give me a year at the American Academy in Rome. There was a pause.

I had to say something. Anything. I blurted out, "If my memory serves me, you yourself got this same award."

"No. I never got it."

"Well, keep plugging!"

He did not laugh. The conversation soon ended. I found out years later why Cheever had chosen not to be amused. When his inimitable biographer, Blake Bailey, called me about an unrelated matter, I told him about my remark. He explained the silence that had greeted my presumed witticism. Years before the phone call, Cheever, married, his first son born, was desperate for money to support his family. He had been led to believe that he was to be given the Rome Prize, which at that time, would have meant two years of financial security. He didn't get it. It was given to poet John Ciardi. No wonder he hadn't laughed. (This tale is included in the Bailey biography, a footnote on page 223. I am a literary footnote. One takes one's distinctions where one gets them.)

When I returned from Rome to New York, just before New Year's Eve, 1980–81, I was told by Diffy that a gay cancer was going around and that it was expected that five percent of those who had it would die. No one knew what caused it or how to treat it. I should be careful, whatever that meant.

Also, Eddy Parone told me that a friend of his, the writer Larry Kramer, was sending out notices warning gays about what was happening. I asked Eddy to let Larry Kramer, whom I had never met, know that I'd be more than willing to help, even if it meant doing nothing more than licking envelopes. Word came back. "Tell Joe Caldwell that I hated his novel [*In Such Dark Places*] so much that I don't want to have anything to do with him." And I could have become a founding member of Gay Men's Health Crisis!

I was, however, offered another opportunity to be of some use.

The predicted five percent was, before too long, revised to one hundred percent. Pneumocystis carinii pneumonia became the number one killer. Dementia, blindness, as well as the cancer Kaposi's sarcoma were also numbered among the possible afflictions that signaled a person's immune system had been fatally compromised, meaning put out of commission totally and irreversibly.

The number of people diagnosed increased by multiples. Twenty-five hundred one year would increase to five thousand the next year and double again the following year. A plague was upon us. At one point, 1982–83, the illness was named: Human Autoimmune Deficiency Syndrome (AIDS). The means of infection became known: not communicable by air or touch but by bodily fluids, primarily blood and semen. Those first infected were drug abusers who shared blood-tainted syringe needles and sexually active homosexuals—semen.

St. Vincent's Hospital, with which I would soon become involved, was in Greenwich Village, at the epicenter of what remained for some time the ground zero of the epidemic It initiated a 110-bed unit reserved for people with AIDS that was quickly occupied. The staff agreed to be assigned, a near-heroic act considering that, despite increased knowledge, uncertainties shadowed one's every move. A needle prick could be a death sentence.

Several things must be mentioned here. St. Vincent's Hospital, whose primary mission was service to the poor—founded, staffed and administered for 162 years by nuns—is no more. It went bankrupt. Its buildings have been demolished. Its often frantic emergency room is gone—even though it had been so vital on September 11, 2001. No public or private rescue of the hospital was effectively attempted. Rumors of consolidation never advanced to reality and whatever efforts might have been made were dead on arrival.

Further, on its leveled site a number of buildings devoted to condominiums for the wealthy were constructed and now provide habitation for their affluent occupants.

At one time a large share of my bitterness was heaped on the blameless head of New York's billionaire

Michael Bloomberg, who was the mayor when Saint Vincent's closed. I went so far as to note that he had at one time rallied the troops—the City Council and the taxpayers—and, from the public coffers, exacted sums sufficient to build a playpen for the enthusiastically revered/reviled New York Yankees in the Bronx, but nothing for a hospital for the poor.

These thoughts, of course, are invalid. St. Vincent's was a Catholic institution. The mayor could no more have rescued it with public funds than he could have rescued the Catholic parishes and schools now being shuttered by the Archdiocese. The one wall to which I heartily subscribe to is the constitutional wall between church and state. It must remain forever impregnable.

So what about the Archdiocese of New York? St. Vincent's was its flagship hospital. My efforts to research the Archdiocese's involvement or noninvolvement have proved futile. It's my surmise that it was already reeling in response to the legal actions being taken against it by victims of sexual abuse and had no resources left for a foundering hospital.

My last sad thought is that the condominiums and the history of the site upon which they have risen give an accurate measure of what the city I once so deeply loved and where I could live paying a twenty-four-dollar-per-month rent, has now become. And it is my uncharitable and, in all likelihood, futile hope that the occupants of these condos never be allowed to forget that the land on which they have staked their privileged claim will forever be holy ground and that they remain aware of their own part in its desecration.

But I can't end this digression on so negative a note. Consider Bellevue Hospital on Manhattan's First Avenue. It's still standing, a lasting and thriving monument to New York's insistent resolve that no needy person will ever be turned away for want of funds to cover the cost. I should meditate on this more often.

During the mid-eighties, an old acquaintance, Bill Hoffman, had his AIDS play, *As Is*, produced by Circle Rep on Sheridan Square; it then moved to Broadway. It was an effective play, especially since it dealt knowingly with the epidemic and had a fearless (for the time) compassion for those caught up in its devastation.

However—and note the emphatic italics—the play's narrator/commentator is an ex-nun, a woman who, consistent with her calling, initiates a useful and compassionate response to the epidemic. Laudable to say the least. I repeat my *however*. The play makes a significant point of the nun's expulsion from her convent and from her order. She is, by inference if not by outright association, involving herself with gays. What could be a more legitimate reason for banishment?

The simple truth is that at St. Vincent's, not more than four blocks north of Sheridan Square, where the play was being performed to considerable acclaim, a real, live nun, Sister Patrice Murphy, had already put in place a hospice program for those with AIDS—*with the full cooperation of her Order and her hospital.* It provided each person taken into the program with a nurse to assure that inpatient or outpatient medical care was available and a professional social worker to provide guidance through the tangle of social services and offer counseling if needed. Then, finally, it offered a nonprofessional volunteer whose attentions, it was hoped, would to some degree diminish the experience of abandonment suffered by most of the patients, the repudiation by family, the avoidance of longtime friends, and the general isolation the illness exacted.

These rejections were not always in response to the illness itself. A diagnosis in most instances revealed the patient to be either gay or a drug abuser or both—social categories that justified at that time immediate scorn and lasting repudiation. These people were only getting what they deserved: blindness, dementia, a disfiguring cancer, cystic lungs—all leading to an inevitable and lonely death. To counter this, the volunteer would offer friendly companionship and, if needed, physical and emotional help. The training for this consisted of a series of evening sessions and some Saturday mornings. It covered a wide range of orientation, knowledge, and instruction, much-needed preparation for what the volunteer would be doing after being assigned to a patient with whom he or she would be involved until the patient's death. (After a respectful interval, a new assignment would be made.)

A guiding principle of the volunteer's relationship

to the patient was consolidated into four words: "no demands, no expectations." Likability was not an issue, whether it be the patient for the volunteer or the volunteer for the patient. Gratitude was beside the point. Service, defined by the patient's needs, whatever they might be, was the one and only guide. Whatever evolved, whatever developed, would be what it would be—but the "no demands, no expectations" rule was ever applicable.

This I know because, by 1985, the epidemic had continued to grow, decimating the gay community. I wanted to do more than just wring my hands and weep or even pray. The Sunday newsletter at my parish church, now St. Joseph in Greenwich Village, included one Sunday a notice regarding the volunteer organization at St. Vincent's. (Soon the hospice program was required to change its name because "hospice" legally applied only to those whose life expectancy did not exceed six months. Some patients were living longer. It became the Supportive Care Program.)

It is amazing what it does to a relationship when you enter into it with "no demands, no expectations." You're not passive; you're just less intrusive. It's all about the patient. You respond rather than initiate. For me, there would be ten of them, each one unfailingly interesting; some more complicated than others. Caring was never a difficulty. And I found that I had a knack for it and remained committed to the cause, with an unwavering focus on each patient that prevented me from wondering about who the next one might be.

In one of the training sessions, an authority on the subject of grief lectured us at length on the ways to deal with it. I was not unacquainted with loss. He told us to trace on a piece of paper he'd provided a comparative measure of our sorrows going back to our earliest years, rather like a graph showing the fluctuations of the stock market.

While my father, my mother, my sister Franny, and my nephew Tommy had all died, I began with a childhood sorrow so pervasive and so unrelenting that I was, at the time, both surprised and quietly amazed that I could feel so deeply. No previous or subsequent loss or disappointment had reached down to such a depth into the heretofore unknown recesses of my being and placed there a grief so great that it forced me to know myself in a completely different way. Life could no longer be the same after that. It was like a loss of innocence.

I was in sixth grade and about eleven years old. Until then I had been protected from this new knowledge about myself and from the ferocity of what I was capable of feeling. Shameful as it may seem, of all the peaks on the graph recording subsequent losses, none surpassed this first height.

Our dog, Hookey, had been run over and killed by a car. My mother made the announcement when I came home from serving as altar boy for the early Mass. That I immediately burst into tears surprised my mother. After all, I was not only eleven, I was a boy. She told me the details. Hookey had been out front chasing alongside a car on Twentieth Street in front of our house and had been caught beneath a back wheel. The driver had stopped and moved her close to the curbstone in front of the Carrigans' house farther down the block, nearer to Kilbourn Avenue. My mother had covered her with a small throw rug so that my older sisters, Rosebud and Helen Margaret, would not see her when they went to school. Later the Humane Society, our ASPCA in Milwaukee at the time, would come and take her away.

I went to school. I joined my class, still in church for the daily Mass from which I was exempt because of my earlier service. I began to cry. My classmates were confused. After we left the church, Sister Annette questioned me and I told her, sobbing, what had happened. She was not exactly indifferent, but she was less than impressed. Later, at recess, I cried again. She was now sympathetic, but still puzzled by what she obviously considered peculiar behavior. To Sister Annette, as to my mother, I was eleven years old and a boy. I shouldn't cry.

How long did my grieving last? I feel it even now as I write these words.

This was the first time in my life that a devastation that might assault me could not be corrected or assuaged by my mother. I was introduced to the limits of what her love could do. No consolation was possible. The loss of innocence comes in many forms.

About some of my patients.

My first patient, Jeff, an African-American, age twenty-nine, stuck in St. Vincent's because he couldn't be discharged without some place where he could stay. There was a chance he could be admitted to Bailey House, a residence for people with AIDS in the renovated Christopher Hotel on the corner of West Street and Christopher, right on the Hudson River, but first he would have to go there for an interview. He refused to go. He didn't have a decent overcoat. It was January and he was too proud to wear the tattered garment he'd been wearing when he came into the hospital.

Jeff had a degree in business administration from Baruch College and, for a time, had worked in some administrative capacity for Macy's. But he had become a drug abuser. Someone had turned him on to drugs at a friend's Christmas party more than a year ago. I managed to get him an overcoat from Don, the head writer from *Love of Life*. It fit. He got into Bailey House.

I'd visit him three or four times a week. He told me about how his mother had thrown him out of their apartment because of the drugs. He stole. From his brother, from his sisters, from his mother. He had a girlfriend he hadn't seen for a while. He had bought her a skirt and went to see her. Her mother informed him that she had died. Of AIDS. (Had he infected her?)

One day I got a call from Bailey House. Jeff was acting strangely. I rushed down just as he was running out the door onto the street. He moved quickly up the block. I had to run to catch up and to keep up. He was in a rage. He was crying. "I'm back on drugs!" he shouted. "I went back! Go away! Leave me be! Go away!" He picked up speed and I thought it best for now to let him go. What could I have done? As was the case so many times, I was helpless.

He went into detox in a locked ward at Beth Israel Hospital. I was the only person allowed to visit him: not even a family member would be admitted. When I went to see him, I brought him his favorite food: Chinese egg rolls with hot mustard. He seemed to be doing well and we chatted a bit before he asked me to sneak him some cigarettes, which were forbidden by the detox program. It was a desperate plea. I said nothing.

I had noticed, however, that when I went to the desk before being admitted to the locked ward, they paid no attention to the paper bag I was carrying with the egg rolls. I could sneak in the cigarettes.

I talked to no one in Supportive Care about the request. I'd have to make this decision by myself. What I finally realized was that if I were to bring him the cigarettes, his respect for me would diminish. He would know that I could be manipulated.

I went to see him. I didn't tell him that truth. I told him another: that the cigarettes might threaten his health and I would never forgive myself for that. He told me he understood. I was not to feel bad. He then spent the entire visit making me feel bad.

Then there was my patient Bruce, who insisted he be called Montana. I complied as did everyone else, including his family. He, too, was living in Bailey House. He liked to shop. I'd get him the necessary wheelchair and we'd head out to the nearest supermarket, where he'd spend most of the food stamps he'd been allotted on specialties like chopped chicken liver, thinly sliced prosciutto di Parma, and smoked salmon. Several times I did supermarket shopping for him: fresh fruit (especially strawberries and melon), quilted toilet paper—superior to the Bailey House brand—and Very Berry fruit drink, paying with food stamps. At first I was embarrassed, but I soon convinced myself that food stamps were nothing to apologize for or to be ashamed of. (I'm a writer. I may be in need of them myself someday.)

On other wheelchair excursions, we'd go to the St. Luke's Thrift Shop on Hudson Street and he'd buy brightly colored neckties, not to wear, but to bring some cheer to his somewhat Spartan room. To do what I could to improve the décor, I gave him my large beach towel with broad stripes of yellow and purple. He tacked it onto the wall as if it were a medieval tapestry. Our most extended wheelchair journey was to a shop on Eighth Street near Fifth Avenue, the one place in the world where, he claimed, he could buy with money from a cash fund he said was his burial money, a special imported coffeemaker.

He must have spent all of his burial money at one time or another because, at his death, I had to go to some municipal office in Brooklyn to arrange for a payment to be made to Reddin's Funeral Home on West Fourteenth Street—which, by the way, was, during the epidemic, one of the few—or possibly the *only*—mortuary to provide services to those who died of AIDS.

I can't tell you how much I enjoyed Montana's insistences. My all-time favorite was a request he made when I told him I'd be gone for a week or so for a family reunion in Wisconsin and I asked him if he'd like another volunteer while I was away. He did. It should be, he insisted, a white gay male.

When I reported this to Carole, the head of the volunteer program, she said, very much in character, "We're not in the habit of asking our volunteers if they're white."

Finally, I'll tell you two of his most characteristic questions: "Why can't I do it?" and "Why can't I have it?" And I myself had better have an adequate answer.

One patient proved to be different from all the others. Not long after I was introduced to Tom I realized that he and his friend and caregiver, Michael, were both unfailingly interesting, each in his own particular way. Tom's defining characteristic, besides being amiable and intelligent, was a strong sense of entitlement, whereas Michael's defining characteristic, besides being amiable and intelligent, was an uncomplaining response to his friend's near-limitless requests.

During the time I was involved with them, they were living together on the comfortable second floor of a house in the Bronx owned by Michael's agreeable mother, who lived downstairs. Tom, of course, no longer had a job but had inherited a certain amount of money after the death of his lover John. He therefore spent a great deal of time going through catalogues from which he would order whole inventories of supplies—food, drink, toiletries, kitchen accessories, including two ice cream-making machines, the second more sophisticated than the first.

Michael worked the night shift at a nearby hospital. Often, when he'd come home, Tom would present him with his requests for the day—usually starting with a visit to a supermarket.

The sizable freezer compartment of their refrigerator was stocked literally to overflowing. The door, to be secured, had to have strips of duct tape stretched across it and onto the sides of the refrigerator.

This made sense to me. Consciously or subconsciously, Tom was providing himself with needs for an extended future—an understandable rejection of his present situation.

Then there was Tom's insistence that part of the backyard be transformed into a patio, the space defined by some red bricks carefully placed into the dug earth. A small pool was also required—with running water, yet! I helped, but Michael did most of the work.

It was a given that I would join them when they came into Manhattan for doctor's appointments and outpatient medical procedures. I would also spend Sunday afternoons with them, most often visiting in the living room, I with a cup of Earl Grey tea. On several occasions Michael would drive us to a quaint town in the countryside for lunch. On the way home, Tom would want to stop in a supermarket. Other times we'd bask in the backyard patio in the shade of a convenient tree. Our conversation was easy and usually cheerful—since our first purpose was to amuse rather than inform.

But when did Michael sleep? I never asked and he never approached the subject.

Tom's most extravagant act of entitlement came toward the end. He tried to steal a very expensive Hermès scarf from Bloomingdale's department store. He simply exchanged the scarf he was wearing for the one he preferred. He never made it to the door.

It was, of course, Michael who took charge. (I wasn't involved and only heard about this later.) He pleaded for clemency, noting that Tom was dying. Whether the judge was compassionate or decided not to burden the prison system with the care of an inmate with AIDS, I do not know. But it can't be too difficult to guess which of the two was operative.

Tom died at home.

Michael was relieved of all responsibilities and his reward was an inconsolable grief that, I am sure, still resides somewhere in the deepest reaches of his unconditional heart.

At some point during our time together I mentioned to Michael that his name in Hebrew asks the question "Who is like God?" With a wicked smile stretched across his handsome face, Michael lifted his arms away from his sides and held out his open hands, presenting himself to me. "Now we know," he said.

If, as has been proclaimed, "God is Love," Michael wasn't far off the mark.

Of all the varying experiences I had with my patients, my time with Bobby was the saddest. I'd been aware that each patient seemed to have an inner resource that might help sustain him through the days and nights. Jeff had his pride. Tom and Montana had their sense of entitlement. Bobby had his mother.

Bobby was the youngest in the family, with three older sisters. When I was assigned to him, he was still living with his mother and one of his sisters, Cookie. In his twenties, he was very much his mother's favorite. In truth, it would be more accurate than insulting to say he was still his mother's baby. Short in stature, Bobby was slightly pudgy, with a sometimes elfin disposition that found its expression in teasing people. (In the hospital: "I seen you sneaking into your bathroom to hide and smoke a cigarette!") Not a great wit, but he did make us smile.

Then, midway during our time together, his mother died. A major part of his grieving was his confusion. He seemed never to be sure of who he was. It may have been that his mother's caring and her ever-present love defined him to himself. If so, now he was lost. And his sisters, who, by the way, had promised their dying mother that they "would take care of Bobby" wasted no time breaking their promise.

When Bobby had been in St. Vincent's, very seldom did his sisters ever come to visit. There was, however, one cousin, Mary, an attractive woman who came often and was always cheerful, but in no way able or obligated to take on Bobby's care after his mother's death. As for Cookie, I knew from a previous experience what her response would be about caring for her brother.

Bobby was staying with her in their mother's house. He had fallen in the bathroom and hit his head against a cabinet. There had been a lot of blood, and Cookie had had to clean it up—*very* carefully. It was infected with HIV and exposure in the smallest cut would be fatal. It was decided that Bobby should come back to the hospital. An ambulance would be sent.

Meanwhile, Carole, the nurse in charge of volunteers, drove to his house located in the far reaches of Brooklyn and agreed to take me along, so we could offer whatever help might be needed.

Bobby was resting in bed, his head swathed in a clean towel. Cookie had done a good job. I had been with Bobby for only a few minutes when Cookie appeared in the doorway to the bedroom. "You're not coming back here!" she all but shouted. "You're going to a facility!"

Bobby went into complete tantrum mode, his fists beating the mattress at his sides, his feet kicking the air while he howled a "Nooo!!!" that began in his throat and reached into his forehead. I did what I could to calm him. I was close to succeeding when Cookie reappeared in the doorway. "You're not coming back here!" she repeated more forcefully than before. "You're going into a facility!" Again, she disappeared. Again the tantrum and howling returned. So much for Cookie. But who, ultimately, could blame her?

Of the two remaining sisters, one cited her children as a reason for not bringing someone with AIDS into her house. Understandable enough. As for the third, it was Bobby who rejected the offer even before it was made. He explained to me that her husband would come on to him, wanting sex. I pointed out, "But you have AIDS." Bobby immediately let me know that this would not be a deterrent. And that settled that.

Bobby did go to a "facility" after all, Rivington House on Manhattan's Lower East Side. I went to see him as frequently as I could. None of my patients had been as abandoned as he was.

At times, to relieve the monotony of the Rivington confines, I'd take him for dinner at an inexpensive greasy spoon down the block where, at some moments, remnants of his elfin self would begin to surface. Other times, at his request, I'd bring him his favorite dish, spaghetti with plain tomato sauce—a selection I never understood. Once it was from a Chinese restaurant—lo mein, whatever that is.

The only "resource" available to him now was cigarettes. In his unit, there was a room of some size with a window for its fourth wall. It had a special vent and was offered as the one place where smoking was allowed. Almost every time I came to visit, I would find Bobby in the ventilated space. He and the other smokers were too busy puffing away to establish much comradery.

The first few times I visited him, I would, so he wouldn't feel neglected, join him. Soon enough I came to feel that the vent was not all that effective. Bobby and those in charge disagreed, but on further visits I'd wait in his room—sometimes for more than just a few minutes. But I persisted in visiting without complaint about the long waits, my occupation during them being my sadness. He had no one. He had nothing, except cigarettes, which, I admit without apology or excuses, I willingly provided.

Toward the end, my visits followed a near formulaic scenario. I'd try to get a conversation going, but almost unfailingly my pauses allowed Bobby to mutter in flattened tones, "Get me out of here." I'd try to continue the so-called conversation with more "Blah, blah, blah." Again, like a mantra, "Get me out of here."

Never was I more inadequate.

When Bobby died, Carole and I went to the funeral and his sisters proved to be genuine mourners.

I was with my next patient, Marty, the longest: two and a half years. He was a talented young man who had designed and built in his apartment a loft bed that one reached by a winding staircase. Cabinets. Track lighting. His anger was never far below the surface—much of it at himself for what was happening, but there were others who managed to excite his wrath.

When I was first assigned to him, his mother was visiting him from Salt Lake City. She was magnificent. "This is not going to get you! We're not going to let it!" She prescribed a special tea which she would supply and that he must take regularly. What was happening to others would not happen to him. She went back home to Salt Lake City.

When I commented to Marty how extraordinary his mother was, he corrected my assessment by recalling to me an event that had taken place during her stay. He and his mother were about to sit down to the dinner that she had prepared when she asked him if he had a tape measure.

Puzzled, he said, "Yes," and then sat down at the table.

"Can you get it for me?"

"Mother, we're just about to eat."

"I know, but can you get it for me?"

"It's in the back of the closet. Let's eat."

"No, get it for me. Please."

"What do you want it for?"

"I want to measure your couch to see if it will fit in my den."

How the conversation ended, Marty never said.

Marty had a close friend, Arnold, who did not have AIDS. Sometimes Arnold would be taking care of Marty and I'd be taking care of Arnold since Marty's complaints, his dissatisfactions could at times be overwhelming, even to a close friend.

He refused the professional caregiver sent to him through his insurance company. He refused him because the man was fat. He fired the nurse from the Supportive Care Program who, to this day, has not the slightest idea why. Except it's obvious. He had to lash out at someone. Anyone. He had an unending fight with his landlord, putting his rent money in escrow until certain improvements were made to the apartment. His rages gave him energy. The money was still in the bank when he died. It went with the rest of whatever he had to his friend Arnold.

Arnold, too, was often the object of his anger, usually for no reason. At one time, when Arnold and I were walking away after spending some time with him, he said to me wistfully, "And I used to be the difficult one."

And yet, of all the untimely deaths I experienced in those fifteen years, the death of my very first patient, Jeff, was the most difficult. This was probably because he, more than any of the other patients, challenged my determination to apply "no demands, no expectations." His pride made him highly unpredictable. Once, because he felt slighted, he got dressed and left the hospital without being discharged. He was soon readmitted but had to go through all the admissions procedures—physical, X-rays, questionnaires, and more—all of which he angrily objected to. Then there was his return to drugs and his King Lear–like rage against himself. At another point he refused a visit from his mother because she'd thrown him out. Still, there was somewhere in his pride a latent dignity which I couldn't fail to sense. And, finally, toward the end, an innate kindness managed to rise and assert itself.

One evening during his final hospital stay I brought

him the six-pack of lemonade he'd asked for. Immediately he gave one can to the patient in the next bed and another to the man visiting him. Still another went to the woman who took away his dinner tray. He did drink one himself while I was there, after I'd repeatedly declined his offer of one for me.

Also around this time I did his laundry at my local laundromat, and while I was folding it at home before bringing it to him, I found myself pressing a clutchful of his clothes close to my chest, holding it there for a few seconds.

Two nights later he told me I had been like a brother to him. Then he died.

10.

I did take one break from the Supportive Care Program and that was to go for a residence at the Mac-Dowell Colony. I'd come up with an idea for a new novel based on the time I spent in Rome reaping the reward of the prize I'd won.

It had been the Academy's policy to give each fellow an extra chunk of money along with his or her monthly stipend in the January of the fellow's year, an encouragement to travel around Italy. We were there, after all, to acquaint ourselves as much as possible with the limitless riches of Italy's contribution to our Western culture. I was expected not only to write my novel, but to leave my studio, get away from the Academy, even abandon Rome itself and experience as much of Italy's cultural heritage as could be crowded into my allotted time. I needed little encouragement.

Even in my studio, a small, cabin-like structure, two

walls of which were the bricks of an ancient Roman wall, I would often ask myself: "What should I do to-day? Should I work on my wretched little novel or go down the Janiculum Hill, through Trastevere, across the Tiber, and take another look at some Caravaggios? Or perhaps climb the Aventine Hill and spend some time in the sixth-century church of Santa Sabina? Or head for the coffee bar in Piazza San Cosimato, where I could, undetected, play the native by having a late-morning cappuccino?

My explorations outside of Rome were mostly to the south—to Naples, to Sicily. Eventually I narrowed them down to Naples, a city whose energy spins the world. To me, who could never decipher their dialect, the Neapol-itans were objects of endless fascination, especially their physicality, their movements, their gestures. No body part was exempt from being called into service for some expressive need. Wrists and knees were particularly use-ful, but it was the hands, the hands that did most of the work—grabbing, pinching, groping—a finger tugging down a lower eyelid, four fingers thrust sideways into the mouth, thumb and forefinger joined, both hands giv-en a series of shakes to let the listener know that some annoyance demanded immediate correction.

To prepare myself for one particular visit, I read a book about some traditional Neapolitan customs, one of which dramatized their legendary concern with status, with how they presented themselves to each other and to the world at large. For an important event—a wedding, a funeral, a First Communion—a distinguished gentleman would, if no other candidate was available, be paid to attend. He would then with casual confidentiality be pointed out as "the uncle from Rome." This would, in turn, elevate the event to a gathering of some importance. This importance was applicable to each of the guests without exception and promoted a general sense of self-approval bestowing upon the occasion a distinction that guaranteed success and earned for the host an eager approbation.

Whether this custom is still in practice among present-day Neapolitans, I do not know. Nor do I care. I'm a fiction writer and it's my job to create a believable world in which convincing situations are acted out by interesting and, if possible, compelling characters.

So back to my idea. What if an American who speaks an assured Italian with an assured Roman accent would, as a favor he could not dismiss, present himself at a Neapolitan family gathering, a wedding to be more specific, and be introduced as "the uncle from Rome"?

And so I spent a month in Naples by myself—observing, exploring, deciding very specifically where each scene would take place, even noting in which direction the traffic was moving on a particular street.

And once I returned, I offered this idea to my imagination—the ultimate arbiter as to whether or not a novel is lurking somewhere within. I was given not just permission to proceed, but a demand. At the

MacDowell Colony that spring, I went to work. My main character was a middle-aged opera singer who was having a well-respected career singing *comprimario* or "character" roles. Having studied and trained in Rome, his accent was perfect, a perfection made possible by the highly sensitive ear necessary to a man of his calling.

My imagination suggested he have a longtime obsession with a long-ago-lost love. As if I were doing research, I became obsessively interested in a fellow colonist at MacDowell who remained completely unaware of my interest, no matter how much charm and wit were dispensed in the effort. That he was decidedly heterosexual was not allowed to be a consideration. An obsession is an obsession (see Proust).

To give the unimpressionable young man one final chance to claim the prize, I decided when I got back to New York I'd get tickets to the then current Broadway production of O'Neill's early comedy, *Ah Wilderness!* and late tragedy, *Long Day's Journey into Night* and invite him as my guest.

I got the tickets. Then sanity intervened—before I could take the final steps toward idiocy. I realized that the fellow colonist was actually a surrogate obsession and definitely not the true object of my impossible yearnings. That was and would always be Gale/Bill. I said to myself, "Why not take the risk? Why not invite him?" It certainly would be the more honest thing to do. So, after a fifteen-year hiatus, I phoned him. I invited him. He accepted.

Then he said, "I should tell you. I have AIDS." Before I could react or respond, he continued, "I've aged. A lot. And I've lost some hair. Then there are these lesions, sort of like bruises, from what's called Karposi's sarcoma. But they're more aggressive. Kind of like skin cancer."

Obviously, he was warning me that he looked exactly like what he was: a man with AIDS, and did I still want to invite him? Which gave me a needed context to say something about what I'd been hearing. "Do you feel up to going?" I asked, then quickly added, "I hope so."

"Sure," he said. Then to my astonishment, he added, "I feel fine."

And so it was agreed we'd go together. Because of my understandable concern I almost asked if I could come to see him before then, but some instinctive warning suggested I settle for seeing the play together and let it go at that. Which is what I did.

A few days before we were scheduled to meet at the theater, he called to say he was going through another siege of feeling just plain lousy. I asked if there was anything I could do, not mentioning the volunteer work I was doing. He declined the offer but said he had a doctor's appointment the following week at Bellevue Hospital, just a few blocks from my apartment. He'd stop by. I mentioned my apartment was a fifth-floor walkup—implying that this might be a difficulty. He repeated, "I'll stop by."

My bell rang. I buzzed him in, then went into the hall and down one flight. A bald-headed man was on his way up. "Bill?" By no stretch of the imagination could this have been my longtime acquaintance, but I'd prepared myself for almost anything. The bald man continued up. Bill appeared on the steps below me. I had not been adequately prepared.

Not by Bill, not by my three years of experience at the hospital. Aged he was, and he'd lost most of his hair. But it was the Kaposi's lesions on his face that forced me to suppress a gasp. It was as if the face had been splattered with thrown mud, and, in retaliation for the indignity, he had refused to wipe it off. Any difficulty he may have had with the stairs was disguised by a measured pace. His greeting had a note of wry amusement, the exact words I've now forgotten—a way of saying, in effect, "What do you think of the changes?" What I answered is also forgotten, but I hope it gave no hint of how appalled I was at what I was seeing.

In the apartment, we went into what had earlier been a living room but was now dominated by my desk rather than a couch, the cramped corner in the bedroom never having been conducive to a writer's restlessness. He took the rocking chair. (Remember the rocker, the play I wrathfully wrote for my friend, Eddy?) I sat in my reading chair by the window.

It was fall and the weather was a New York autumn at its best. We talked as if less than a week had passed since our last get-together. AIDS was not discussed. He'd bought a house on Staten Island; he'd been teaching photography at Pratt Institute in Brooklyn, but not for the past semester or two—the single (and oblique) reference to his condition. Since it was lunchtime I offered to go and get some pizza in the shop downstairs. He preferred that we eat there. It was a very specific indication that proved to be a rule—that he would never avoid appearing in public. He refused to be intimidated by his splotched face.

We had pizza. The conversation was cheerful. No matter how he looked, it was good to see him. I walked him to the subway on Twenty-Eighth Street. At Park Avenue South, he pointed across the street and said, "Look at the woman in the blue dress standing next to the green mailbox." And there, indeed, was a woman of no distinction clad in a cotton dress of deepest royal blue, standing next to a dull green mailbox. The artist's eye. Seeing what no one else sees.

THE ENDING

11.

Bill was hospitalized again at Bellevue. I went to visit. I kissed him on the forehead. He had no reaction. It may have been during this visit that I mentioned my volunteer work, but it could have been later. Some still small voice warned me—in no uncertain terms—not to be more than casual in our renewed acquaintance.

While I was there, what must have been a resident doctor came into the room with about five young interns or, perhaps, students. The doctor introduced himself and asked Bill if the intrusion was okay. It was. The doctor's express purpose was to give his charges a glimpse of Bill's lesions. It was, he said, the most excessive explosion of the sarcoma he'd ever seen, an example of how the cancer could run rampant and uncontrolled throughout the entire body when the immune system had been so thoroughly disabled. Would Bill please take off his pajama top?

Bill got out of bed most willingly and, as if to treat the spectators to the sight of a rare and astonishing marvel, he took off his top. The students failed to disguise their horrified amazement. Bill's back, chest, and arms were covered with a mass of lesions. There seemed to be no space left for even one more. The doctor did not comment. He thanked Bill. They left. Bill put the pajama top back on and got into bed. We resumed our conversation.

When I got up to leave, I made a movement toward giving him another forehead kiss by way of farewell. He put up his right hand to fend me off. "One kiss per customer," he said. I accepted the admonishment with a half laugh.

Not long after, I went to his home on Staten Island, an uphill walk from the St. George ferry. The house was set on a double lot, meaning that there was a side yard equal in length and width to the space taken up by the house and its own backyard, which extended to what I judged to be over a hundred feet. The house itself was a two-story frame, painted tan with brown trim. A small grape arbor separated the front side yard from the back, providing shade as well as grapes (in season) for the birds to feast on. All of this was presided over by a cherry tree, huge for its species.

Originally Bill had intended the second floor of the

house to be a rental apartment providing a reliable income. With his native skills he'd renovated the space and, for a short time, had had a tenant. No one lived there anymore. He didn't like the footsteps over his head.

Because he'd concentrated on refurbishing the upstairs, his own quarters on the first floor and in the basement were still in a primitive state. What was meant to be the living room was a warehouse, a depository for the countless boxes of his books, odd pieces of furniture, some still unpacked clothing, and a five- by five-foot chest of shallow drawers suitable for stowing what I think were oversized sheets of treated paper that probably related to his photography. Somewhere in the jumble his invaluable cameras were hidden away in places never to be revealed, even to me. (I was invited to guess, and failed—which made him very proud.) There was also a cot-sized mattress on the floor. Near it, against the wall, was my Hague Street Franklin stove, no longer in use.

Called into service as an impromptu living room was a space less than half that given over to storage. It managed to accommodate a glass-fronted bookcase, well stocked, one easy chair plus another chair less capacious but comfortable enough, and a sturdy table with legs ornamented by what looked like swollen kneecaps. The table was large enough to hold the radio/stereo, a digital clock, and a cleared area big enough for writing. In a corner near the doorway to the bedroom was a cardboard carton strong enough to support a stereo speaker. The carpet was of a forgettable design and the two windows faced the backyard, actually the garden, planted mostly with tomatoes and shaded by the out-sized cherry tree.

The bedroom was given over almost completely to a double bed (which, incidentally, the Italians, with an uncharacteristically straight face, call a *matrimoniale*). Shelves tightly lined with books rose from the bedside to the ceiling. A television set partly blocked the window overlooking the yard.

In the basement were a refrigerator, a stove, a washing machine and dryer. Also, stacked lumber that would never become a fence separating the side yard from the sidewalk, household implements including a vacuum cleaner shaped like a huge bass drum (which sounded, when in use, like a low-flying jet), and jum-bo-sized bags of dry dog food for the stray dog Bill had semi-adopted and respectfully named Mr. Dog.

Nowhere did I see any evidence of a darkroom.

On my second visit I must already have mentioned my St. Vincent affiliation and described what it involved because, at one point, he asked, "Am I a project?"

I was thrown by the question. Was he? I recovered sufficiently to arrive at an acceptable truth. "No. You're my old friend Bill." He was satisfied.

My then-current St. Vincent's patient, Marty, was going through an encouraging period of fairly good health and had his friend, Arnold, who would let me know of any reverses. I was therefore completely

JOSEPH CALDWELL

available to Bill for what would be the eight-month duration of his illness—and made myself not so much "available" as simply present, like a friend enjoying his companionship.

Careful not to be too importuning, I would phone ahead and ask if it would be all right to come visit. Very rarely did he say he'd prefer I come another time. After a few of these rather soft-spoken requests he finally said, "You ask so timidly. Why not just tell me you're coming—and then come?" Newly resolute, I did as instructed, and seldom did he decline.

Soon my sense that he was adamantly opposed to any emotional involvement with any of the people around him became a certainty. Very, *very* definitely, under no circumstances whatsoever, was I to declare my deeper feelings. The last thing I would be allowed to say was "No matter the ravages of the sarcoma that disfigures your entire body, you're still the most desirable man on the face of the earth." I came to this realization about overt emotional statements through his disdainful comments about a woman who had been a student of his at Pratt, Marilyn. "If I were to ask her to jump off the Brooklyn Bridge, she'd jump." Marilyn was desperately in love with him.

From all this, I was forcefully informed that to declare one's love for Bill was to invite a scornful contempt, as if an unforgivable demand was being made by some hapless suppliant. With reference to my own experience, my thinking was this: It was allowed for

Bill to initiate an intimacy. If initiated by someone not of his choosing, the rejection was infused with ridicule, his contemptuous dismissal absolute and beyond appeal. Applied to my own case, going back all those years, I could finally understand why any effort I might have made to rekindle his interest would have been doomed from the start. I would be making a demand. One did not make demands. I was reminded of the advice given at the start of my volunteer training: no demands, no expectations. This was quickly put into practice, and Bill, as the evidence suggests, seemed to remain none the wiser.

And we did have projects from time to time, each demonstrating distinctions and differences between our two natures: his extremely competent and mindfully patient, mine completely unskilled and impetuously heedless.

The tomatoes had already been harvested, the freezer stocked with enough zip-lock bags of spaghetti sauce to feed a family extending two generations past and two generations to come. One day, in among the denuded stalks, the two of us were doing something or other preparing for the colder months ahead. There were planks between the planted beds. Bill explained that he had aerated the soil, digging down a couple of feet, the better to nourish the vegetables. So as not to tamp down the laboriously aerated earth, I was instructed to walk only on the planks. I nodded. I understood.

Within minutes I heard Bill say rather calmly,

"You're stepping on the soil." I moved onto the planks. Not that much time had passed before I again heard Bill's voice, "You're off the planks again." We finished our task, but not before Bill's admonishment, patient and resigned, was repeated at least one more time.

The roof leaked. We went up to repair it. To get there we had to shove open a ceiling trapdoor on the second floor, reached by climbing a not especially re- liable ladder, get through a crawl space, and hoist our- selves onto the roof—a flat slant, higher at the front of the house. Bill went first. I handed up the bucket of tar, the tar of a consistency that made possible spreading rather like frosting a cake. I handed up the sheet of tarpaper and an exceedingly aggressive scissors. I then hoisted myself onto the roof.

"Don't step on the bubbles," he told me. This, I gather, was so I wouldn't get tar on the soles of my shoes and bring it into the house.

Bill located the place where he thought the leak was coming from, identified by judging where the rain water had been coming through the ceiling of the up- stairs apartment. Gray plastic trays that looked like oversized dish pans that he had used in his darkroom, had collected the water. Scissors and tar paper in hand, I went to join him.

"You're stepping on the bubbles."

"Oh. Sorry."

He nailed down the tar paper and sealed it with the tar. I watched. The job was soon finished and seemed expertly done. Bill had a competence that I truly admired. He decided that the trays would stay in place, checked after every rainfall. Not a single drop ever appeared.

On the way back to the trapdoor, I gave Bill the opportunity to say one more time, "You're stepping on the bubbles." I took off my shoes before stepping onto the ladder.

There was the fence to be built along the sidewalk. We began by sinking the posts that would be held in place by some stones reinforced with poured cement. We each had a spade. The posts were already shaped according to the design Bill had decided upon.

Bill dug his posthole. I dug mine. His was neatly done, each side of the hole straight down, forming a perfect cubic space. Mine looked like a hole a dog might dig to bury a bone, as if I'd clawed away the earth with my paws. The hole's circumference at the top was twice the measurement needed, the sides uneven slopes, the bottom a tiny point that could accommodate little more than a pin tip. I dug deeper to provide adequate space for the actual post. But then my post would rise to a lower height than Bill's.

With a few well-placed shoves of his spade, Bill made right all I had done wrong. Surely we were meant to be the perfect couple. (The two planted posts were all that we would get to do to build the fence he'd so handsomely designed.)

Later that fall Bill was back in Bellevue. He was having gastrointestinal problems. Around this time he explained why he was being treated at Bellevue and not at a Staten Island hospital. He'd had no health insurance at the time of his diagnosis. If he'd been tested for the virus a few months sooner, his predicament would have been quite different. At that time he would have been covered by the benefits accorded the full-time faculty at Pratt. But that was then, and the time had come when he should have been put up for tenure. He had been advised, however, by some administrative staff member, not to apply that year. As I understand it, he was told that it was Pratt's policy to accept no more than two applicants a year for tenure. The two other faculty members eligible were both women, and affirmative action, more or less at that time, assured their acceptance.

Bill was advised to revise his status to adjunct for the following academic year, then revert to full-time the year after, when his chances would be sufficiently improved. This meant a reduced salary and no benefits. It was a sensible proposition and he made the necessary arrangements. The rest of the story needn't be told.

As far as I could tell, Bill felt no bitterness or, if he did, he kept it to himself—just as he kept any bitterness about his illness a private matter. He seemed incapable of self-pity, and the reconciliation of himself to what had happened, what was happening now, and what would eventually happen was, and quite possibly would remain forever, known only by William Gale Gedney. Up to a point.

When Bill was discharged from Bellevue, a young and attractive nun from a Staten Island convent, Sister Kate, was there to drive him home. She was a "buddy" assigned to Bill through Gay Men's Health Crisis (*Peace*, Bill Hoffman!). I was on hand. Sister Kate was bright and cheerful. We were enjoying the ride to the island over the Verrazano Bridge when Bill, in the back seat, warned that an attack of diarrhea was coming on. Sister Kate picked up speed, but it was too late. Bill suffered the indignity of soiling himself and the back seat of the car. (Later he commented: "I've never done that in a nun's car before.") He was distressed; Kate and I managed to be unfazed professionals. I got Bill inside; Kate said she'd take care of the back seat.

Another person I met was an Englishwoman, Recenda Kramer, a Staten Islander and another GMHC volunteer. Her sense of humor was crisp and to the point. Before I'd been initiated into the domestic chores requiring instruction, such as operating Bill's washing machine, she insisted on doing Bill's laundry. He was reluctant to impose and claimed that it wasn't necessary, even though he was bedridden at the time. Her reply: "I've *seen* your sheets." She was allowed to proceed.

Sometime in November, Bill went through an exceptionally tough time: fever, and nausea. He was being given Bactrim. I was staying over, sleeping on the mattress in the storage room, my nose twelve inches from my defining Hague Street relic, the Franklin stove. If Bill needed anything during the night, he would knock on the wall. Sometimes he would complain of dry mouth. From that time on, an ice bucket with a can of ginger ale was at his bedside.

His fever got worse. 104. A Staten Island doctor came. He lowered the dose of Bactrim. The nausea disappeared. The fever was gone.

For me, some of our better times were when we'd go in Bill's van to an enormous supermarket (measured in acreage) a few miles away. The shared domesticity pleased me. One of the items Bill would buy was a wheat something-or-other that one bought in bulk, measuring for oneself with a scoop, pouring it into a bag. This gave him a wicked pleasure. Although he never touched the wheat, he enjoyed the notion that other customers might be horrified if they'd seen him—sarcoma and all—scooping up the exposed wheat.

He cooked. I cooked. Once I made a pasta and, not being sufficiently attentive to the recipe, I put the tablespoon of salt intended for the boiling water in which the pasta would be cooked, into the sauce, which already had olives and capers. It was inedible. Other times I was more efficient, with meatloaf, a noodle casserole, other recipes for pasta. (About the meatloaf: Bill instructed me in tones firm and resolute that, at the butcher, I was to order stew beef. After the man had cut the beef into chunks, only then should I ask that it be ground up. The butcher was not to be trusted. I complied. But once I put in too many bread crumbs. We had crumb-loaf.)

Bill on another occasion made what he called a Swedish pancake. I watched. As he proceeded, I told him it was really Yorkshire pudding. I was told that I was wrong. It was a Swedish pancake. Our competitive natures asserted themselves briefly, and I gave in. For the time being.

For Christmas, Recenda invited us over for dinner. There were other guests and none seemed bothered by Bill's appearance. One odd moment, however, a pleasant woman, ample and blond, of a few more than middle years, was talking to me about Staten Island. She mentioned the neighborhood where she'd grown up. It was Bill's neighborhood. I asked her the address. It was Bill's address. We asked her if she wanted to come to the house. "No," she said. "It would only make me cry."

The dinner itself was very enjoyable. Cheerful conversation, wine (which Bill and I declined), a superfluity of vegetables and, Recenda being English, roast beef and Yorkshire pudding. In tones of simple curiosity I blandly asked, "What's the recipe?" She listed the ingredients and the method of preparation. We were eating a Swedish pancake. I glanced at Bill. He managed to be otherwise engaged.

From our shopping excursions I learned of Bill's attraction to a bargain. It boosted his morale to find something at a reduced price. He felt somewhat cheated to have to pay the full amount. The value of everything was determined by how big a bargain it was. He read newspaper ads, something it had never occurred to me to do. He found that Altman's, the respected but then failing department store on Fifth Avenue, was offering flannel sheets at a price close to theft. Gleefully, I was dispatched. I bought the requested sheets and delivered them with the receipt—evidence of his triumph.

Once I bought some shrimp. Bill liked shrimp but thought them too expensive. To assure his enjoyment, I lied about the price. He was most approving. So pleased was he that he mentioned the shrimp—and the price—to a visiting colleague from Pratt. Impressed, she asked where I got them. A practiced liar, I told her they were a one-day special.

Make fun of his parsimonious nature as I may, he'd managed to buy a house. And he owned a van. And any number of valuable cameras. I had a typewriter, a television, and a stereo.

Bill's condition deteriorated. No great crisis, just diminished energy and high fevers requiring more bedrest. A few months into the New Year, 1989, a decision had to be made. If the deterioration continued, would he have to be hospitalized, at some point permanently? The alternative was hospice care at home under the auspices of Staten Island's Richmond Hospital—available when the patient was judged to have entered the final six months of life. Only palliative treatment would be given.

There would, of course, have to be a qualified home caregiver. In that circumstance, his health would be monitored by an assigned doctor and nurse who would make scheduled visits. Because of my training at St. Vincent's I was qualified. No matter his condition, Bill could stay at home in his own house. I would live with him. I would be there full-time, sleeping on the mattress, watched over by the Franklin stove.

Easily we occupied ourselves. A voracious reader, he was working his way through Dickens, having arrived at *Dombey and Son*. I would work on the Neapolitan novel I'd begun at the MacDowell Colony the previous summer. At first I used Bill's typewriter, but when I began to worry about it being noisy and disruptive, I switched to longhand in a notebook. It made a difference to Bill that he could see me writing, that he wasn't keeping me from my work.

Bill wasn't all that much of an invalid at the time of the hospice assessment. Shared tasks and an occasional excursion were still possible. There was a show of paintings by Courbet at the Brooklyn Museum. Some other friends of Bill's, including his Pratt associate Nina Prantiss, arranged, with the help of Sister Kate, to get about six of us there to see the exhibition. The dominant painting was a huge canvas of two women on a tousled bed, one lying down, the other kneeling near her on the bedclothes. To me it suggested the moment immediately after lovemaking, the two of them seen in a state of placid satiety. To Bill I said, "Yes. That's the way it's supposed to be"—expecting him to elaborate on the subject. I could then refer to lovemaking, to its satisfactions, to the languorous moments that might follow. It was my hope that this, in turn, would lead to some reference, some reminders of our own time together. Until then, I had, as I've mentioned, never introduced the subject.

But here was a pretext to approach it and see where it might lead. Where that might be, I preferred not to consider. A sexual involvement was out of the question. Bill had already told me that fortunately all his sexual desires had vanished completely, and even I was not stupid enough to even entertain the possibility. What I probably half hoped for was some degree of renewal of our emotional intimacy. I even thought that he himself might retrieve some measure of our distant beginnings and the memories might soften and make less diffi- cult his present condition. I wouldn't be just a friend; I would be a loving friend. A pretext introducing this absurdity had presented itself and I had accepted the opportunity. Now it was up to him.

His response was simple. What I had said was obvi- ously of no interest. It deserved no elaboration. It wasn't even deserving of a dismissal. A dismissal would have implied consideration. In effect, he hadn't even heard me. His thoughts were elsewhere and he felt no need to articulate them, much less to involve me in their development. Upon reflection, this was the preferred resolution. No demands. No expectations. All foolish, stupid, and preposterous impulses must not only be re- sisted, they must be completely avoided. And if I didn't like it, well, as we used to say, tough titty.

It's said that animals, pets in particular, have a sense that makes them responsive to a "master's" physical or emotional condition. Mr. Dog, who had seldom been allowed upstairs from the basement and had always been put outside at night, began to come around less and less. Bill attributed this to his inability to play outside with the dog the way he used to. And now he had even passed the responsibility of feeding him on to me, which was hardly a chore.

I claim to be a dog lover, but Mr. Dog, a German shepherd mix, and I never managed to, as they say, "bond." True, I never threw a ball for him to fetch, but I did pet him and tickle him behind the ears. He was not responsive. Once in a while when he sat next to me as I read in the backyard, he'd nuzzle his snout under my hand, lifting it so I could give a couple of strokes along his neck, down along his back, and pull his tail, but not all that often.

As had been his habit from the beginning, he would wander off most of the day and appear erratically. When Bill had been going through a time that required more bedrest, I let Mr. Dog upstairs. He raced up the basement steps and into Bill's bedroom. He leaped onto the bed. Bill, thrilled to see him, laughed and laughed until he was almost screaming. Mr. Dog dove under him, around him, licking his face, whining and whimpering in ecstasy. He crouched on the blanket at the foot of the bed, then lunged forward and dug his snout between the pillow and Bill's right ear. Bill yelped with joy.

I watched. I was jealous. Of a dog.

Eventually even my shouted calls in the yard, "Mr. Dog! Mr. Dog!" failed to summon him. Day after day, evening after evening, my words went out for the entire neighborhood to hear, but no Mr. Dog bounded up to me to accept the bowl at my feet. My shouting sessions became a sometime event. Then I gave up. "He's not my dog anymore," Bill said.

Gradually I got to do things few Manhattanites get a chance to do. I cut the grass. The so-called lawn mower was, to me, a strange implement. It had no wheels, no blades. Powered by a thick electric cord that snaked its way out the basement door and into the side yard, it was a handheld rod with string at the tip. Turned on, the string whipped in a blurred circle with a ferocity that, without mercy, lopped off the top of any blade of grass grown too tall to be tolerated. Its whirr made a single-note low nasal whine, warning the hapless grass of its approach, vengeful beyond appeal and pitiless in its execution. I very much enjoyed cutting the grass.

I shoveled snow. The sidewalk wasn't that long, but this was yet another exotic exercise available to homeowners, and I appreciated the opportunity to become reacquainted with what had been an unappreciated childhood chore. And the cold fresh air was invigorating.

I did the laundry, which didn't demand any of the coins required by the laundromat I normally dealt with. And Bill's machine featured sophistications I didn't know were possible. It could wash sweaters. Slowly, gently. Bill had a lot of sweaters. I dutifully ran them through, then, on a bedsheet placed over newspapers spread on the floor of a vacant upstairs room, I'd lay them out carefully so they'd dry without losing their shape.

It was the regular laundry, the sheets especially, that gave me a particular pleasure. Not the washing, but the drying. I'd hang it all out to dry. On a clothesline. With clothespins. In the fresh air, preferably under a benevolent sun. The scent of sun-dried laundry is one of the more beatific smells available on this earth. I can't describe it. I won't even try. It has to be experienced. (My introduction to the phenomenon came on one of my earlier visits. Bill had brought in the dried laundry from the yard. I lifted one of his white sweat socks to my nose. Bill said, "I don't remember giving you permission to smell my socks." My answer, "I didn't think it was necessary.")

Together we planted some flowers along the side of the house. I noted that he'd chosen sweet William to bookend the row. My favorite was hyacinth. In bloom, it gives off a scent almost as inviting as sun-dried laundry. And I found it a more reliable effusion (for want of a better word) than that given off by a rose. A rose is undependable. Hyacinth never disappoints. I'd bring a blossom into the house and have a sniff whenever the urge asserted itself.

For all of Bill's love for flowers, he felt nothing but

annoyance when a huge bouquet arrived with a card signed by Marilyn, the former student who'd committed the unpardonable error of letting Bill know how much she loved him. "They look like something you'd send to a Mafia funeral," is what he said.

Because the flowers were delivered by the florist, no thanks were offered at the time of delivery. Bill didn't even want them in the bedroom, where, by then, he was spending more and more of his time. He had me put them in the living room, out of his line of vision. When Marilyn phoned and asked me—Bill was sleeping—if the flowers had arrived, I not only told her that they had, but that he was thrilled by them and had them next to the bed.

There were entertainments. On the TV we watched *The Golden Girls*. We also watched old movies, the two of us propped up in the bed with pillows at our back. Bill introduced me to a lesser, but fascinating, Anna Magnani film called *Bellissima* about a Roman mother who tried to get her little girl cast in a movie being filmed at Cinecittà. The mother, by coincidence, sees the director, the producers, and casting staff watching the child's screen test. The little girl is crying, helpless, frightened. Those watching find it hilarious. The mother, outraged, lets the unfeeling film people have it—Magnani style—the scene that justified the movie's existence.

Another movie we saw was *Airplane*—a satire of catastrophe movies—the first in a genre that would later include films by the Zucker brothers and the *Naked Gun* franchise.

From my friend Ron Sproat, a film enthusiast, I borrowed *My Cousin Vinny*, *When Harry Met Sally*, and, on another level, *Odd Man Out*. The first two, intelligent and enjoyable comedies, made for some very pleasant evenings. *Odd Man Out* was a less felicitous choice—for reasons that became more obvious while we were watching it. A man (James Mason), allied to an organization (not specified in the film but obviously the Irish Republican Army in Northern Ireland), helps carry out a successful robbery but is shot before he can make it into the getaway car. The film then becomes the tale of a man wounded, dying, searching for someone to help him, to take him in.

His political attachment makes him an untouchable. No one dares help him as he tries to find his way to his friends. Near the end, he poses for a mad artist who had taken him in for the grotesque purpose of capturing on canvas the face of a dying man. As we watched, I realized: not a proper choice.

Bill, rather than dismiss or resent it or allow himself to be notably affected by the film's content, concentrated on the camerawork, commenting with genuine admiration for the imagination and expertise of the director and cameramen.

I also read to him, mostly from a book of ancient Chinese tales set down centuries ago and recently translated. I learned there and then where Saturday matinee movie serials came from—each episode ended with the main character or characters imperiled beyond rescue, a rescue that would begin the next episode.

The tales were enchanting and I had the added pleasure of sitting on the bed next to Bill as I read. (One time, with reference to no incident in particular, Bill said, "I can smell you on the pillow next to me." "Does it bother you?" "No. I like it.")

Close to an entire afternoon (or so it seemed) was spent listening to tapes Bill had made of songs by Rodgers and Hart and by Cole Porter. What distinguished the tapes—aside from the genius of the songwriters— was that each song was sung no fewer than three times, with a different singer and a different arrangement, exploring the song's interpretive possibilities.

Fortunately, Mr. Hart and Mr. Porter were the chosen lyricists. The vaunted sophistication, the wordplay, the ingenious unpredictable rhymes, the boastful cynicism, as well as the surprising diversity of interpretation, rescued the repetitions from being the musical equivalent of Chinese water torture (think Philip Glass, etc.). Still, it was a long, long tape, seeming at times to have no promise of an ending. Bill enjoyed himself immensely, sitting there in his chair, at times tapping his toes or crossing his ankles in dance steps of his own invention. I could have done with a little Mozart spaced at regular intervals. This was not to be.

Bill loved those songs. His devotion was absolute. His appetite for their inimitable treasures was beyond satiation. I remembered Charles Ives, Bill's obsession, the time we devoted—I mean *devoted*—to listening to record after record of his incomparable compositions.

Where was Ives now? Where were Piston and Sessions? Even Barber and William Schuman? The pantheon had been emptied. New occupants inhabited it now—Rodgers and Hart and Cole Porter. As I've already observed, Bill's enthusiasms were so intense, so absolute, that they could not possibly be sustained. Relief was necessary, change inevitable. How well I knew. How well I knew.

Lorenz Hart turned up again at a later date, even more necessary and appreciated. Before I'd moved from the mattress in the storeroom to a quilt at Bill's bedside, I was awakened one night by the sound of Bill singing to himself. I considered going to him, but these seemed sounds of easy contentment, an assist in passing some wakeful moments that had interrupted an otherwise uneventful night.

I mentioned the singing the next morning. Bill had had, he told me, a nightmare. It consisted of nothing more than the sight of a stretched gray line. But it had terrified him to the point of waking him up. To ward off the terror that had followed him into his waking state, he'd decided to sing to himself the lyrics of Lorenz Hart. That's what I'd heard. That's what had happened. Hart had been present and ready to help. Bravo Lorenz!

It wasn't often that Bill showed me his photographs. When he did, none was current because he wasn't doing any photographing, nor, as far as I could tell, had he done any for quite a while. This was uncharacteristic of the Gale I'd known. Photography was central to his life. It was how he defined himself. Now, however, the house with the finished apartment upstairs, with the flourishing garden outside, with the plans to build a personally designed fence—with all this, a darkroom had not been included among his achievements or among his plans, which dated back a few years. I never introduced the subject and he never referred to it. However, the photographs he did show me may hold some clue to his neglect.

His pictures from India, from Benares and Calcutta, had been published in a slim paperback book. They were extraordinary because they were quite ordinary: the Indian people doing what Indian people do. Pulling carts, selling their wares, avoiding ambling cows, sleeping in public, diving, swimming, staring into the camera. The pictures were free of an agenda. He had been documenting no previous conceptions; he had no interest in politics or protest. Poverty in India was rampant, but it didn't seem to be of concern to those he photographed—the poor themselves—and he made it of no concern to himself. Not from personal indifference, but from an artistic standard that made no allowances for melodrama or sentimentality. Bill's own humanity was free of self-dramatization; he responded empathically, it seemed, to those who neither demanded nor expected special attention. As with any artist, knowingly or not, he revealed himself in his art.

There had been a fairly reliable possibility that the photographs would be published in a deluxe edition by a highly respected house with a foreword by Raghubir Singh, the noted Indian photographer. It would have established Bill as a photographer worthy of attention, important to an ascendant career. Nothing came of it.

In his will, Bill deeded his cameras to qualified Indian photographers who couldn't possibly afford them, probably chosen by Raghubir Singh. In a ceremonial moment arranged by Bill's brother, the American ambassador to India handed them over to the Indian ambassador to America.

The other series he showed me he kept in a sort of scrapbook or photo album. They were pictures of the more famous composers of the day, taken in places familiar to them: the woods near a country home, at the piano, walking a dog. Almost casual, deceptively so. The revered without the reverence. Homely almost—in the true sense of its root word, "home"—without an effort at being homely. Copland, Piston, Carter, and many more.

The nonportraits had been intended as part of a book—Bill's photographs with a text by a well-known authority. He never named him. In any event, the project fell through. The text writer's dilatory or waning interest somewhere along the line, the publisher's, the editor's? Who knows? Not I.

What I can't help wondering was (is) this: Could Bill have become so discouraged by these disappointments that he suffered a photographer's equivalent of writer's block? Although his San Francisco series—1960s hippies of Haight-Ashbury renown—had been shown at New York's Museum of Modern Art, his subsequent series had been ignored: Myrtle Avenue before the El was torn down and the Village-like neighborhood destroyed; the Appalachian family that would—after his death—be shown at the San Francisco Museum of Contemporary Art (150 photographs in all) to a very favorable reception. There were other series of which I'm unaware. He was now well into middle age. Even though he had no instinct for self-promotion, he did have—I don't doubt—a sure sense of his own worth and the artistic value of the work he'd done. There is no way to verify this speculation, but it persists. Posthumous regard is all well and good, but a little upfront might have been helpful from time to time. Don't forget, artists are people, too.

At times Bill would talk about some friends (or lovers) who had at one time or another been important to him. On this subject, Bill once spoke of an extremely satisfying six-month involvement with an Italian-American who had since moved to California. I asked Bill if he wanted to get in touch with him. His answer was an oft-repeated phrase when referring to past acquaintances: "He must be dead by now." The epidemic was like that.

If this memoir of mine gives the impression that Bill, by whatever private means, had stoically accepted what was happening to him, that impression should be slightly altered. True, he showed little bitterness and less self-pity. He occupied his days with activities for as long as he was able: his house, his garden, easy companionship with colleagues like Nina Prantiss, Peter Bellamy, and other friends from Pratt. Later, reading, music, movies—all with little or no complaint.

On one occasion, however, he touched on a serious subject, but chose to make fun of it. One morning, when I was giving him his pills, he mentioned that he'd recently considered swallowing all his prescription medicines, bringing the whole difficulty to an end. Then he said, "But with my luck I know I'd just wake up with one big headache."

On other occasions, an obviously suppressed rage erupted and gave some measure to his deeper turmoil, both of them questions to which there were no answers. "Why wasn't I born a eunuch!?" And closer to the end, "Why can't I die!?" As there were no answers then, there are no answers now. Exclamation points as well as question marks. That's the way he said them—angry, bitter.

Medically untrained and uninformed by the attending doctor, I had no specific knowledge of his prognosis other than that AIDS was eventually fatal. In the doctor's defense, I never asked. Something the nurse said suggested that the cancerous sarcoma had attacked his interior organs, as opposed to its relentless attack on that exterior organ, his skin. If so, the word "attack" should be amended to "nibble"—a slower, more insidious assault, a quiet feeding rather than a savage gnawing, less apparent but no less effective. Still, the suffering was there, the unappeasable discomfort, and the palliative care he was being given offered very limited relief.

So much of the time I was concentrating on what had to be done that I could be unmindful of what was going on, what all this was really about: Bill's dying. Yet there would be moments when the full force of reality struck with a blow for which it was impossible to prepare. One such moment occurred when, late at night, Bill woke up (I was sleeping on the quilt on the floor at his bedside by then). He said he wanted to sit up in his chair in the living room. I had to remind him that I was no longer able by myself to give him the help he needed to move that far. So advanced was the illness that he was all but immobilized. I'd have to carry him. Or drag him. The first I couldn't do; the second I wouldn't do. He persisted. He wanted to sit in the chair and nothing else was acceptable. I tried to be as persuasive as I could, but to little effect.

He was patient in his insistence. I was equally patient in my reasoning. I even tried lifting him to show him how inadequate I was. He quieted down and seemed to have reconciled himself to the impossibility of his request. I lay back down. I was almost asleep when I heard Bill grunt, a sound made with great effort. Then another grunt. I got up.

He'd managed to move his body sideways on the

bed and slide himself halfway toward the floor, onto my quilt. What he was doing was, given his condition, heroic. He was refusing to accept the limits imposed by the deterioration he was going through. He was determined that this act of his would prove that he was still who he was: a man faithful to his determination, no matter the difficulties arrayed against him. This was far, far beyond mere stubbornness. It was an assertion of self—and close to the time when he could have that self taken from him forever. Helpless, inadequate to his imperatives, his near-final response was a patient defiance.

All I could say was, "Oh, Bill."

I managed to slide him back onto the bed and straighten him out so his head could rest again on the pillow. He didn't resist. He said nothing. I kissed him goodnight and lay back down. My tears I kept to myself.

The last time Bill was able to get out of bed was after he had sold the van (for a thousand dollars) and Nina, who'd arranged the sale, came over to drive it off. It wouldn't start. He had to get up, go outside and get the ignition to kick in.

But it was a negligible event and unworthy to claim so great a distinction in this narrative. I've chosen as his last experience of the outside air an afternoon in early June when Maria Friedlander came for what would be a final visit. She is the wife of Lee Friedlander, the noted photographer, a good friend of Bill's—as was Maria.

As closely associated as Bill may have been to Lee, I strongly suspect it was Maria who was the more valued friend. It's not all that difficult to elevate the suspicion to an assurance. Considering Maria, the word "lovely" comes first to mind, accompanied by a small smile as I set down the word. Quietly pretty, with long hair and a more than pleasing face, she was, perhaps primarily, with no effort whatsoever, a comforting, understanding, and easily responsive woman. She claimed that Bill had a too-idealized version of who she really was. If so, I confess to an equal inaccuracy, which, I protest, is not inaccurate.

So Maria and Bill could be alone together, I went outside with my notebook, sat on the bench near the basement door that opened onto the yard, and scribbled away at my novel in progress, *The Uncle from Rome*. It was the most perfect June day in history. The flowers were in aggressive bloom, the presiding cherry tree was sending down, like a blessing, a soft fall of white petals that the breeze arbitrarily dispersed throughout the yard. There were certainly enough to go around. I myself was a favored target and not once resented the distraction.

Maria and Bill came out, Bill in his bathrobe and slippers. He wanted to show Maria the results of his plantings. Aside from little more than a nodded acknowledgment, I let them continue their private meeting. But how could I not want to see them in among the tomatoes, Maria no doubt keeping her feet firmly on the planks. Their words were more murmured than

spoken. Out of respect for the intimacy of the occasion, I did my best to concentrate on my work. But the
two of them were more compelling than whatever I
might achieve with my scribblings. Now they were in
the side yard, Maria flicking the leaves of the grape
arbor, then the two of them admiring a bush in the
far corner. Slowly they moved, quietly their murmur-
ings continued, on to the row of flowers along the side
of the house. (Whether purposely or not, Bill seemed to
have ignored the two posts of the never-to-be-completed
fence. It could be that Maria had the good sense not to
ask any questions.)

The sweet Williams, the hyacinths, the other flowers we'd planted fulfilled the purpose for which they'd
been created: Extravagant as they were, they felt no
need to do anything more than exist. It was enough.
Bill knew it. Maria knew it. I knew it.

The soft sifting blossoms from the cherry tree continued. I stopped writing. It was enough. It was enough.

It was obvious that Bill was in his last days, but the
signs went unnoted—not because they were ignored,
dismissed, or denied—but because there were things
to be done. I felt no need to place them into the larger
context of which they were the central part. Little by
little his appetite diminished until he'd eat only fari-
na with chopped strawberries mixed in, or ice cream,
mostly vanilla. After a time these had to be spoon-fed.
Still, he seemed to enjoy them.

Only on one occasion was there a slight difficulty

and that was very much of my own making. He was resisting his medicine but could usually be persuaded. One night after I'd had a busy day, he decided he didn't want to take the sleeping pill the doctor had prescribed. I told him he needed the rest, which was a lie. He was bedridden and slept most of the time. I was the one who needed the sleep. And if he didn't sleep, I didn't sleep. There would be requests: he'd like some hot chocolate. He'd like me to read to him. None of this would I deny him. However, my own lack of sleep made me tired and I felt I'd be less effective the next day.

The night he refused the pill, he later asked for some ice cream. I brought it—but I had slipped the pill inside. I was spooning the ice cream into his mouth. After about three spoonfuls, he gagged and started to reach his fingers into his mouth. "There's a walnut," he complained.

I prefer not to imagine his reaction if he'd discovered the deception. From that day to this, my shame has only increased. It was a betrayal, an act of selfishness at a time when my needs were very much beside the point. My fingers were swifter than his and were into his mouth, retrieving the pill before he could take it into his own hand and see it for what it was.

He was satisfied that the "walnut" had been removed. I spooned in the rest of the ice cream. He went to sleep, the ice cream possibly a more effective soporific than the one I tried to sneak down his throat. I, of course, was the restless one that night.

One day he told me to turn off the television. I told him it was already off. He shouted, "Turn off the television!"

I turned the television on. "See? Now it's on." I turned it off. "See? Now it's off." He was convinced, but I was troubled that he'd experienced some disturbance that had no verifiable source.

Another time he told me to turn off the radio in the living room. That, too, was not on. "It's off."

"Pull the plug! Pull the plug!"

I crawled under the table and pulled the plug. "Okay. I pulled the plug." He was satisfied.

Soon after, he asked me who were all those people in the house. "I'm the only one here."

"The only one?"

"Yes."

"I thought there were a lot of people."

"No, just me." This puzzled him. I could think of nothing to say.

Since his temperature remained frighteningly high, I would put some cold, cold water in a basin, and, with a wash cloth, sponge him down. From the look on his face and the hummed sounds of gratification coming from his mouth, I knew it was giving him some much needed, if temporary, relief. On the day before he died, when I was passing the cloth slowly across his face, under his chin, then across his neck, he arched his head back and hummed an even longer hum. As I was applying the cold cloth to the back of his left hand, he said in a quiet voice, "You're so tender."

"I learned that from you," I said. And I spoke the truth. He neither moved nor said anything more.

Because his condition was so obviously critical, it had been arranged for his brother Dick to fly in from the West. He and Bill had never been all that close. From what Bill told me at an earlier time, a baby brother, all curls and smiles, had too effectively laid claim to all available attention. Then, too, as was necessary, an impregnable barrier had been erected to protect the required secrecy of Bill's sexuality. In an earlier phase of the illness, Dick had come to visit his older brother. This was during the time my own visits were random and not particularly needed. After Dick had been there and gone, Bill reported that it had been, for them both, a deeply significant meeting. "We told each other things we'd never mentioned before." I didn't ask for specifics and they weren't offered. But it was apparent that a long-suppressed affection between the two brothers had finally surfaced and I could see in Bill a degree of relaxation not seen before.

His eagerness for his brother's arrival expressed itself in an oft-repeated phrase, "I'll wait 'til my brother comes," even when his brother's presence would affect in no way any activity I might propose. "I'm going to give you a bath," I'd say. "I'll wait 'til my brother comes." "Let me change your T-shirt." "I'll wait 'til my brother comes."

The day Dick was to be there, a call came from Marion, Dick's wife. Air Force One on an airport tarmac with President George H. W. Bush on board had caused the cancellation of Dick's flight. He would arrive tomorrow.

Bill had been particularly restless that day, a restlessness made evident by an unending series of requests. He had sipped only a few spoonfuls of his morning coffee, most of it spilling down onto his already unpresentable T-shirt. Less than ten minutes later he asked for hot chocolate. Two sips of that were enough. I stayed nearby. Ice cream. Coffee again. And so it went. At one point he decided he'd have some of the pecan pie Nina had brought weeks before, which he'd repeatedly refused and which I'd finished off quite some time ago. Hot chocolate was the chosen substitute—he tasted only sips of it, freshly made, spoon-fed.

A little later, the phone call from Marion came about his brother's delay. The news didn't seem to distress Bill. He was calmer and I let him sleep. I did the laundry. I hung it out on the line. In the bright breezy day it dried by midafternoon. I brought it in, took a few sweet whiffs, folded it and put it away.

Bill wanted nothing to eat and I knew better than to try to force him. I didn't articulate it to myself then, but I articulate it now. Bill, by his first enthusiasm for me, then his withdrawal those thirty years ago, had given me instead of the continuation of the lasting love as first proclaimed, instead of the expected companionship into which it may have evolved, a life of everlasting loss, but also a life of everlasting yearning.

No day came, no day went, during which my longing for him wasn't lurking somewhere within me.

With his defection he had deeded to me an emotional life of infinite riches. "Though nothing can bring back the hour/Of splendour in the grass" (as Wordsworth wrote), the yearning and its attendant inability to settle into mere satisfaction brought with it a never-ending agitation that kept active a constant reaching toward something forever to be desired, forever to be denied. Yearning—that most primal of all emotions, more tenacious than love—still lives even when all hope has fled. What riches. Without end. A gift from him.

Maybe equally important, he'd also given me during all these days with him a generous glimpse into what a shared life might have been like, the unnoted contentments of everyday companionship, the exchange of encouragements, the barely conscious compromises and concessions, the domesticated affection that would suffuse every act.

There is more that should be said. I wanted him to die. Only that would prevent him from leaving me for someone else. Not only had my revered St. Vincent mantra been repealed but its exact opposite put in its place: demand and expectation, both equally unacceptable. Yet another truth must be added to this. I felt neither shame nor guilt.

My defense, if a defense is possible, is that this is a natural, if shameful, human response and I lacked the

IN THE SHADOW OF THE BRIDGE

equipment, moral or psychological, to effect a reversal. In the end, all I can say most sincerely is "Forgive me, Gale. Forgive me, Bill."

That night I decided to sleep next to him instead of on the quilt. He was already asleep. I crawled past him to the far side of the bed and got under the sheet. A few moments later he raised his knees and began moving them toward me. If they touched something unexpected, he'd probably wake up. This I decidedly did not want. I got out of the bed as cautiously as I could. He didn't wake up. I lay down on the quilt by the side of the bed and went to sleep.

A sound like a deep and difficult cough woke me up. "Bill?" Another cough. "Bill?" I got up and stood next to the bed. "Bill?" By the first pale light of morning I could see him there, lying on his back, eyes closed in sleep. The sound came again, a gargled growl that seemed like an impossible try for a deep breath. His chest heaved. The gargled growl came again. Then a stillness.

I sat next to him on the side of the bed. He didn't move. Then it came again, the heaving chest, the desperate attempt to take a breath even if it meant tearing up his throat and gargling his ravaged lungs.

"Bill?"

I waited to hear the sound again. I took his hand and held it in mine. I continued to wait. No movement. No sound. Nothing. He had died.

I kept hold of his hand a little while longer. The

digital clock on the bookshelf above the far side of the bed told me it was five twenty. Ten minutes later than the time on the tower clock the day we'd met thirty years and twenty-nine days before.

I reached up and smoothed his forehead. The fever had begun to recede, or it could have been the cooling sweat from the unrelenting fever. I got up and, bending over him, kissed him lightly on the lips, then on the forehead. I let go of his hand and climbed past him. Again I slipped under the sheet and lay at his side, facing him. I reached over and let my right arm lie gently across his chest. Nothing moved. I went back to sleep.

The world is a very strange place in which to live— made stranger still by the people in it.

ACKNOWLEDGMENTS

For my publisher, Lori Milken, thanks and praise for the continuing survival of Delphinium Books after the untimely death of her friend and co-founder, Cecile Engel. And I thank her as well for my editor, Joseph Olshan, who, for starters, encouraged me to write this book, then gave me the right title to replace the wrong one I'd originally chosen. Then, too, I'm grateful for the relentless scrutiny he gave the text, very much to its benefit, and finally, for his persisting belief in the book itself. I also give thanks for having found my new agent, Caron Knauer, who's not afraid to take risks, and I acknowledge Yaddo for the necessary gift of time and solitude.

I thank as well my faithful first responders who unfailingly made sure that my "work in progress" was actually progressing: Mark Nichols (who encouraged me to write the book), Martha Witt, David Barbour, Debbie Hall, and Daniel D'Arezzo. With all of this, small wonder that I consider myself the most fortunate writer I know.

ABOUT THE AUTHOR

Joseph Caldwell is an acclaimed playwright and novelist who was awarded the *Rome Prize* for Literature by the *American Academy of Arts and Letters*. He is the author of five novels in addition to the Pig Trilogy, a humorous mystery series featuring a crime-solving pig. Caldwell lives in New York City.